Wings Over the Foyle

A History Of Limavady Airfield

WORLD WAR II WRECKOLOGY GROUP

By
JOHN QUINN

Assistant writers; Alan Reilly, Tim Cattley.

Foreword by Squadron Leader Tony Spooner DSO DFC

A WWII Wreckology Group Publication. 1995 ©

Wings Over The Foyle

Copyright © 1995 World War II Irish Wreckology Group (WWII(I)WG)
All rights reserved. No part of this publication may be reproduced
stored or transmitted in any form or by any means, electronic or mechanical
without the prior permission in writing of the publisher, nor be otherwise circulated
in ant other binder or cover other than that which it is being published.

Printed by Shanway Press, 461 Antrim Rd., Belfast, N Ireland

Acknowledgements.

The Authors would like to thank the following for their contribution and help in putting this book together.

The Veterans.

Squadron Leader Tony Spooner, DSO DFC, Squadron Leader Eric Starling, Warrant Officer Rod Pike, Joe Crashaw, Wing Commander Jack Hoskins DSO DFC and Dennis Vorley; all from 221 Squadron. Wing Commander Hunter McGiffin OBE, Flight Lieutenant John Dickson, 502 Squadron and Walter Hopper 120 and 59 Squadrons and John Larkin 7 OTU and 172 Squadron.

We would also like to thank the 221 Squadron Association, Public Records Office Kew Surrey and the RAF Museum, Hendon.

Our acknowledgements, are also given, to the following who assisted in the research into Wellington W5653,.

John Ferguson, Dunree, Co. Donegal; Sean Ferguson, Dunree; Mat Kemmy, Ballyliffen; (The late)Hugh Quirke; John Kearney, Lenan; WWII Wreckology Group members, Robert Taylor and Malcolm Huston; Lincolnshire Free Press; Northern Echo, Yorkshire; Nuneaton Times, Warwickshire.

The contribution of the Limavady people is also much appreciated, Mary Douglas, Derrybeg; Ian Grant, Derrybeg; Lorna Pickett, Moira Boyd, Tommy Huston, Sydney Curry, Limavady; and Antony McCallion, Florance Millar, John Wilson, John Barber, Maisie Reilly(for keeping us in cups of tea) Hugh Mullan and Harry McIlmoyle from Aghanloo.

Wings Over The Foyle

We would also like to thank the following, Margaret Quinn and Shelagh Reilly proof readers; Val Grimble, Ron Parsons Hugh McGratton and 'Real Photos/Military Aircraft Photos.

Thanks also to Limavady Borough Council for their help in publishing this tribute to the memory of all the air-crew who operated out of or trained at Limavady Airfield.

Wings Over The Foyle

Foreword

It gives me much pleasure to write a few words about John Quinn's dedicated efforts.

By writing the wartime history of the RAF Coastal Command station near Limavady which was rushed into being in the dark days of 1940, John is serving posterity well. It was then that Britain stood alone as the defender of Western civilisation or, as our Prime Minister had put it: "We are fighting against evil things."

For John Quinn to be doing this during the era of peace which has descended upon Northern Ireland during 1994/1995 seems singularly appropriate as my memories of RAF Limavady, to which I was twice posted for months at a time, were essentially pleasant and peaceful; in so far as war time can be said to be so.

Then as now good was prevailing. Then as now, we all, both literally and metaphorically, 'spoke the same language' whether we came from the North, the South or from 'Over the Water'.

Much of this book recalls death and disaster but I look upon this unusual book not with excess sadness. I see it as a memorial for those who did their best although falling by the wayside. Moreover this book will serve as their memorial long after John, Tom, Alan and I have joined those who have lost their golden youth on either the Irish hills which surrounded this make shift airfield or were swallowed up by the great ocean which dominated the lives of all who flew from this Coastal Command airfield.

Even those who were lost were dedicated to the cause of winning the greatest battle of the war in Europe: the six year long battle of the Atlantic; upon the outcome of which as Winston Churchill so aptly said "All else, on land, on sea and in the air ultimately depends."

Coastal Command of the RAF no longer even exists but books such as this one will serve as a reminder that it was this often forgotten RAF Command that turned the scales in the six year long struggle against Admiral Dönitz's U-boats. It was men flying from airfields such as Limavady and Ballykelly which forced Admiral Dönitz to eat his pre-war words when he said that: "Aircraft can no more attack a U-boat than a crow attack a mole."

Squadron Leader Tony Spooner DSO DFC
January 1995

Wings Over The Foyle

CRASH SITE OF
WELLINGTON W5653
URRIS MTS CO DONEGAL

Wings Over The Foyle

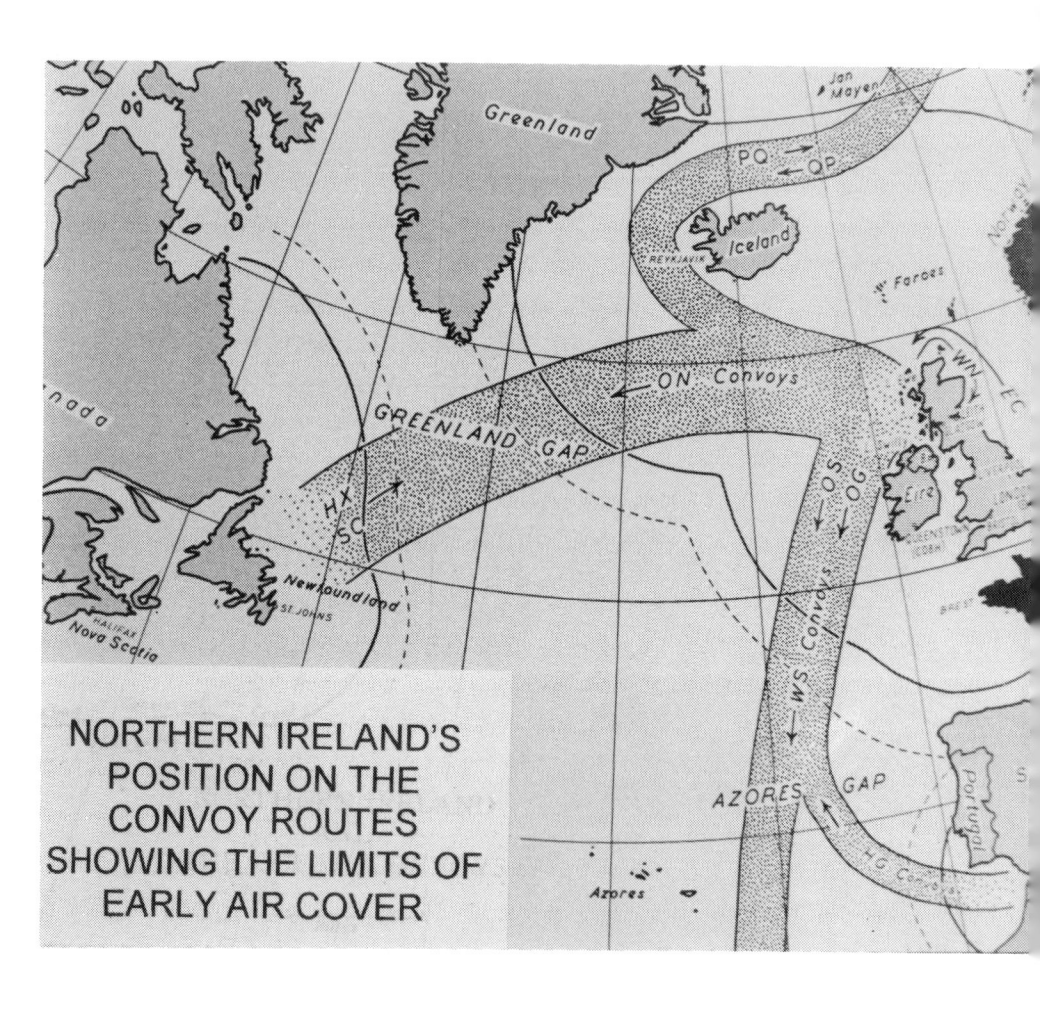

NORTHERN IRELAND'S POSITION ON THE CONVOY ROUTES SHOWING THE LIMITS OF EARLY AIR COVER

Wings Over The Foyle

Preface.

In the late 1930's as Europe slid into another war , it became clear that air power was going to be a major factor in any battle. The 'Battle of the Atlantic' was no different. In order to use aircraft effectively they had to be able to patrol as far out as possible into the ocean. Northern Ireland as the most westerly part of the United Kingdom, was the obvious place to station the aircraft if they were to protect the convoys which were supplying the vital materials of war. Aldergrove, as the only large airfield was not nearly large enough so a rapid expansion plan was implemented which resulted in airfields and flying boat bases being constructed at an accelerated rate all over the province. One of the earliest of these was Limavady or Aghanloo as its known locally. The site, although desirable as it was to the west, was a dangerous one because of the mountains. It closed down as an airfield as soon as was possible after VE day. The subsequent connection that Limavady town had with aircraft was through Ballykelly which was one of the main Coastal Command bases during and after the war. But Limavady airfield was in operation nearly a year before Ballykelly and in the early days of the war it was vital. Many early trials of new equipment were carried out here. Limavady was the front line in the most important battles of the war. This book attempts to highlight that contribution and acknowledges those who operated out of, supported and worked in, this airfield, but mostly it is a tribute to those who died in the 'Battle of The Atlantic'.

John Quinn
Alan Reilly
Tim Cattley 1995

Dedicated to those who lost their life while operating out of Limavady Aerodrome.

Wings Over The Foyle

Contents.

Acknowledgments.	3
Foreword	5
Preface.	9
Contents.	11
Introduction	13
Limavady Airfield County Londonderry;	20
No.245 Squadron	25
No.502 Squadron Operations.	27
No.221 Squadron and the story of Wellington W5653.	34
The Squadron.	34
No221 Squadron Air-crew; 'Seek and Strike'	38
The Story Of Wellington W5653.	45
What Happened On The Night Of 11 April 1941?	55
On The Site Of W5653	66
Flight Lieutenant Eric Starling, 221 Squadron.	76
As the Air-crew Remember It.	78
Local stories	86
The Dogs of War.	93

The Crashes	95
No. 502 Squadron Whitley Crashes.	114
Whitley T4168	121
The Dig On Whitley T4168	123
Crash listings and Roll of Honour.	129
A Listing of Wellington crashes.	129
A list of Whitley crashes;	132
Other Crashes	134
Roll of Honour.	134
References	144
Index.	145

Wings Over The Foyle

Introduction

Winston Churchill said of the Battle Of The Atlantic, "every thing happening elsewhere on land, sea or in the air, depended ultimately on its outcome, and amid all other cares, we viewed its changing fortunes day by day with hope or comprehension."

Britain as an island depended on her sea lanes being kept open, bringing in vital supplies needed to sustain her war effort from the Commonwealth, the Empire and America. It was in fact a lifeline, one that the U boats came very close to cutting, a point that quickly dispelled the pre-war attitude that control of the sea lanes could be maintained by mighty battleships.

In 1940 the situation in the North Atlantic was at a critical stage. The U boats were going through their "happy times" against Britain's merchant shipping, ensuing a casualty rate of frightening proportions. Hitler had failed to bring Britain to her knees in the air war. His invasion barges had been badly mauled in the French channel ports in round the clock sorties by Bomber Command, often at great cost. But unless the carnage at sea could be reversed, the sacrifice paid in the air would have been in vain.

In these early days there were little signs of the forthcoming improvement in joint Naval/Coastal Command tactics and co-operation. However, positive signs did begin to appear as squadrons of bombers made up of American built Hudsons and British Wellingtons were established to rapidly expand Coastal Command. Their purpose, to engage in anti-submarine patrols and provide invaluable air-cover in the western approaches.

Wings Over The Foyle

In Northern Ireland anti U-boat sorties were already underway from Aldergrove, an established pre-war airfield. However the gap where no air-cover existed between east of America and west of the British Isles had to be closed and that meant building airfields as far west in the British Isles as possible. A building program began as several airfields along the north west coast of Northern Ireland began to emerge. Londonderry was already established as a Naval base in the absence of the pre-war naval port of Swilly, Cobh and Berehaven, which had reverted to Irish Free State control.

In March 1941 the first swing against the U-boats emerged and their "happy times" came to an end. The establishment of a Western Approach Command Centre at Derby House in Liverpool, an intensification of Coastal Command patrols, and new convoy tactics caused a significant turning point to emerge.

In this very month 'B' flight of 221 Squadron spearheaded a squadron move to Limavady in Northern Ireland, which at the time was still not fully constructed. In its incomplete state it had to house three squadrons; 502 with Whitleys, 224 with Hudsons and now 221 with their Mk VIII Wellingtons. A detachment of Hurricanes from 245 Squadrons Aldergrove, occasionally used the airfield and detachments of Hudsons from 53 and 500 Squadrons and Whitleys from 612 were also present.

Limavady airfield (locally known as Aghanloo) is situated in the north west of the province along Lough Foyle, twelve miles east of Derry. It was, like many wartime airfields, built through necessity, in terrain far from suitable to wartime flying conditions. This was highlighted by the fact that a mountain, Binevenagh, lay right in the circuit. (Nicknamed Ben Twitch! By Limavady and Ballykelly air-crew) To the west of the airfield lay Lough Foyle

Wings Over The Foyle

and the Donegal hills, to its north Binevenagh and to the east the hills around the Roe Valley, hardly ideal flying conditions!.

When 221 Squadron arrived at Limavady only the runways and perimeter track had been completed. Work had not yet begun on the technical buildings. Temporary wooden huts were used for flying control and operations room offices, and the manor house on the Drenagh Estate became an officers mess. Situated close to Lough Foyle, dampness was a big factor in the temporary buildings, combined with the cold, the wind and the rain made Limavady Airfield a bleak place in 1941.

However, despite the conditions, 221 were not long settling in, as construction continued, operations increased. Aircraft losses did occur, but despite this, 221 Squadron maintained the lowest loss rate per hours flown in coastal command at the time, and their crews built up a pattern of steady experience which became invaluable, and was later injected into other squadrons.

Sir Henry Tizard the man behind Air to Surface Vessel (ASV) radar visited the squadron at Limavady to assess its performance, and from talking to pilots such as Tony Spooner and Eric Starling, he obtained valuable information that would surely have led to improved versions of ASV. No.221 Squadron also carried out experiments in the use of Leigh light used to attack submarines at night.

In June 1941, the first squadron of long range Liberators was established at Nutts Corner near Belfast, under command of a Belfast man, Wing Commander 'Mac' McBratney. This was 120 Squadron, destined to become Coastal Command's top U-boat killers. Men from 221 Squadron were part of the squadron nucleus. Flying Officer Jimmy Procter and crew and Flying Officer Jimmy Ray and crew being the first to transfer. Others such as Tony Spooner were posted to Malta as part of a Wellington 'Special Duties Flight'. Having being billeted in Grant's farm, some three miles from the airfield in the quiet Irish countryside, moving to Malta while his wife returned to London, would surely have proven a big change. (Tony Spooner was later awarded the DSO, and DFC.)

No.221 Squadron established themselves so well at Limavady, that even after the squadron moved to Iceland in September (just as they were beginning to feel at home in Limavady),the squadron continued to maintain its aircraft at Limavady,(in hangers, some of which still stand today). The squadron moved to the Middle East in 1942.

No.502 (Ulster) Squadron, who lost many men in crashes while at Limavady, was formed as a special reserve unit at Aldergrove in 1925. In 1937 with most of the personnel local part-timers they were converted to Coastal Command flying Ansons. By early 1941 Whitleys with ASV radar were flown out of Limavady on Atlantic patrols. The Squadron moved to St. Eval in Cornwall in 1942, where they converted to Halifax's. Their operations from Limavady airfield are included in this book.

No.143 Squadron spent a short period at the airfield with Blenheims.

Many men from all over Britain and the Commonwealth would pass through Limavady. Throughout the war it would remain a "Wellington" base with No 7 Coastal Operational Training Unit (OTU) being there between April 42 to January 44, followed by operations again with two Canadian squadrons 407 & 612, and 172 Squadron RAF.

Wings Over The Foyle

Squadron Leader Walter Zigmond (now deceased) of 221 Squadron, remembered trips to the beaches at Portrush on days off. Rod Pike another former 221 Squadron crewman, later a Warrant officer (navigator), with 59 Squadron was part of the crew that sank U844 on October 16th 1943, remembers drinking in the Alexander Arms Hotel in the town, and also remembers those days off to Portrush. Some of the Rod Pikes crew-mates were later killed when Liberator FL977 of 59 Squadron crashed into Binevenagh mountain on the 24th June 1944 killing all on board.

The World War II Irish Wreckology Group erected a cross on the crash site on the 50th anniversary.

The battle of the Atlantic was without doubt, a hard won victory, won with much suffering. One veteran described the 50th anniversary commemorations, as about remembering old friends, many who died to achieve that victory.

For the Germans too - a high price, 28,000 U-boat crewmen died of the approximate 40,000 who served; 781 U-boats sank, aircraft accounting for more than did surface ships.

RAF coastal command were not credited the same glory as attributed to fighter pilots, or bomber command; yet it was these men, flying long and often boring patrols, keeping the U-Boats down, that held, then secured Britain's lifeline.

In graveyards all over N. Ireland lie the remains of many good men, from all over the British Commonwealth. The majority died in crashes, victims of poor weather and hostile terrain, but also as a result of enemy action.

This small book is a tribute to them all.

17

Wings Over The Foyle

Top;   518/40 Control Tower. Now A Decayed Shell.
Bottom; Bellman Hangers, Once The Home Of Wellingtons

Wings Over The Foyle

Top; The view from the top turret of Walter Zigmond's Wellington 221 Squadron, over-flying the Donegal corridor.

Bottom; A 'stickleback' Wellington MkVIII of 221 Squadron taken at Limavady July 1941.

Wings Over The Foyle

Limavady Airfield County Londonderry;

Should ever an example be sought of the layout of a wartime airfield, then the view from the top of the control tower at Limavady must be the ideal vantage point. Today this one time wartime Coastal Command base reveals an interesting collection of buildings with some unique remains. The tower, lived in after the war, is a 518/40 type and was still in a good state of preservation until 1990. The power plant which once served the active airfield remains intact amid a variety of other buildings which include three Bellman hangers, motor transport (MT) sheds, workshops and dome trainers.

However the most interesting building remaining today is the operation block. Kept locked by the owner, the result is its unique remains have been saved from vandalism. A copy of the station standing orders still adheres to the wall. Traces of warnings of the importance of alertness to loose talk, in the form of cartoon type stickers can be seen in the one times offices. But the most exciting survival is the operations board for 224, 502 and 407 Squadrons. A timeless sight is the names chalked on 407 board, still in excellent condition. No.407 Squadron did two tours at Limavady in 1944 sinking a U-boat on each occasion. If these were not enough two wall murals, one being a Mk III Gremlin are to be seen in a workshop and a Queen Mary trailer and wartime petrol bowser (a one time converted muck spreader) completes the atmosphere as they sit decaying outside one of the hangers.

Limavady airfield is sited two miles north of the town. It was a strange site with a range of hills topped by Binevenagh at 1260 ft rising in the circuit. It was to prove a rather unfortunate obstacle in poor weather and when night flying, especially with Operation Training Units (OTU) crews.

The initial site survey for Limavady aerodrome was in 1938 and construction approval was given in the same year at an estimated £500,000 Construction started in August 1939, (i.e. before declaration of war) the initial purpose was as an armaments training and coastal reconnaissance base. The station was opened in September 1940 and the first recorded use came in December 1940 when "A" Flight of 502 (Ulster) Auxiliary Squadron Whitleys arrived on 27 January 1941 sharing with detachments of 272 Squadron on Blenheims and 224 with Hudsons.

The very early days it was a makeshift arrangement for everything and more than one ex-Limavady airman described the site as a 'sea of mud'. The ground crew had to carry out maintenance in the open in wind and rain, and in the very early days the operations room was a public house in Limavady, possibly because it had a telephone!.

While there 502 carried out several attacks on U-boats, two examples being Flying Officer J.A.Walker who severely damaged a U-boat U93, three hundred miles N W of Ireland on February 11th 1941. His Whitley was damaged in the attack and he landed back at Aldergrove. Another example is Flying Officer Holdsworth who made two attacks on U-boats in four days, one of which resulted in the first 'kill' using ASV. No.502 Squadron eventually moved in January 1942 to Chivenor then to Bircham Newton and on to St. Eval in Cornwall where it converted to Halifaxes staying in that area until near the wars end. It chalked up several U-boat sinkings.

The first Wellingtons to arrive came in April 1941 when "B" Flight of 221 Squadron arrived from Bircham Newton in advance of a squadron moved to Limavady the following month. No.221 Squadron's Wellingtons were equipped with the new Air to Surface radar (ASV. see page 61) deemed most urgent in the Atlantic war. A tragic incident occurred on good Friday 11th April 1941 when one of the "B" flight aircraft W5653 crashed in poor weather conditions into the Urris Hills at 1500 hrs. All the crew were killed instantly. (This site was visited several times during November and December 1989 while researching W5653 and is now recorded in this book).No.221 Squadron stayed until September 1941 and had an active five month tour. During July alone they flew ninety two sorties, attacked four U-boats (two in one day) and had two air combats. During this time three Wellingtons those of Flying Officer Sanderson, Flight Lieutenant Cakebread and Pilot Officer Johnson, were lost. By the end of 1941-502 and 221 Squadrons and detachments of 217, 272, 53, and 500 Squadrons had served in Limavady.

No.7 (C) OTU was formed at Limavady on 1st April 1942 equipped with Wellingtons. The airfield now embarked upon two years of General Reconnaissance and Air to Surface Vessel (ASV.) radar training. With so many over water flights in poor weather and with high ground on its circuit the OTU's own accident rate was high, losing three aircraft in one night 2nd and 3rd January 1943. A local church graveyard -Drumachose bears witness to the losses of Limavady's Wellington crews, a listing of which is included in this book.

No7 OTU moved to Haverfordwest in south Wales at the beginning of January 1944 after nearly two years at Limavady and the station returned to operations with 612 Squadron RCAF arriving with Wellingtons XIV's from Chivenor. While here on

Wings Over The Foyle

10 February 1944, Pilot officer Paytner sank U545. No.407 Squadron had also arrived in January and they also had a possible kill in February. Both squadrons were gone by April 1944, and through the summer the Fleet Air Arm used the base.

However in September both Squadrons returned along with 172 Squadron; 407 had another "kill" in 31st December when U772 was sunk. No.172 Squadron stayed at Limavady, flying patrols until it disbanded on 4 June 1945.

Limavady closed as an operational station in November 1946 but was used by Fleet Air Arm units from Eglinton during the late 40's and 50's flying Fairey Gannets and Chance-Vought Corsairs.

Its present state today is part industrial and minor housing, its runways are largely intact, three of its Bellman hangers remain and the technical site is largely intact but *owned privately with admission strictly controlled.* It has a sense of timeless atmosphere which I found electric and despite some sixteen visits I get drawn back and always seem to discover something new to photograph.

Wings Over The Foyle

Top: Local workers on the airfield 1941 (Photo, N McGonigal)

Bottom: The runway today. Binevenagh stills stands sentinel but bombers no more rumble off this tarmac.

24

No.245 Squadron

Although No.245 Squadron were based at Aldergrove in 1941 flying Hurricanes, there were times when sections flew to Limavady as the necessity arose. On 13 March 1941 No.245 Squadron Operations Record Book(ORB) states " The ruling (13 group operational instruction No 16) calling for sections to operate from Limavady on occasions was today cancelled." They would fly to Limavady when needed and then return to Aldergrove. In March 1941, in response to enemy activity, a section was sent to Limavady on three different occasions, such as that on the 9th when a FW 200 Condor was reported, no contact occurred.

Some other extracts from the operations record book of 245 Squadron make interesting reading and have relevance to Limavady.

On 28 May 1941 at 06.02 hrs a section co-operated with a mobile army column near Antrim. The same afternoon a Blue Section, consisting of Sergeant Hill in Hurricane P3428 and a Czech Sergeant Scrom in W9202, was detailed to intercept an enemy aircraft flying over Eire but no contact was made. In the evening the Squadron was ordered to escort a number of Naval units returning from the Bismarck engagement. Four sections (8 aircraft) were ordered up between 21.00 and 23.30 hrs; no enemy contact was made. Blue section, Sergeants Hill and Scrom landed at Limavady and stayed the night there.

May 29 1941 Blue section left Limavady at 09.00 hrs and on the way to Aldergrove intercepted an enemy aircraft at 18,000 ft south west of Lough Neagh. Hill and Scrom chased the enemy aircraft south as far as Dublin, but were unable to bring it down before their ammunition was expended. They set its port engine on fire however and it is ranked as "probable".

No.502 Squadron Operations.

No.502 (Ulster) Squadron RAF(Aux) 'A' Flight moved to Limavady from Aldergrove on December 1940 prior to a full Squadron move on 27 January 1941. Their Whitleys were equipped with the new ASV. radar, (the first in Coastal Command) and the Mk.9 Bomb sight. No.502 Squadron joined detachments of 272 Squadron on Blenheims, and 224 with Hudsons.

The first experiments with air to ground radar were carried out in various airfields in Britain and 502 crew were involved. Pilot Officer Hunter McGiffin was sent to Christchurch from their base in Aldergrove where the Whitley was fitted with 'special installations'. His log book records flights with Whitley T4141 and a gentleman named Hinkley at Squires Gate doing experimental work. On another occasion on Whitley T4223 flying from Leuchars, he tested equipment designed to detect submarines underwater. The equipment, a large cylinder in the fuselage, only reacted when the aircraft and the submarine were practically on top of one another, so that gear was scrapped.

The Squadron when at Limavady used the old school house, where the community centre now stands at Aghanloo, as a crew room, and the aircraft were maintained in the open. If the wind direction changed during the night and as the perimeter track had not yet been completed, the crew had to taxi the Whitleys up one runway and down the other to again face into the wind before takeoff. In these conditions aircraft left to patrol hours out in the Atlantic.

'A' flight had already lost an aircraft on 23 January, when the crew of T4168 had to bale out due to lack of fuel, three of the crew were drowned in Lough Foyle. The same day 223 Squadron, who were based at Aldergrove, lost a Hudson when it force landed in Co. Sligo. The crew, uninjured in the incident, were interned and the aircraft became the Irish President's personal transport.

The previous month on 21 December 1940, No. 272 Squadron from Aldergrove, lost Blenheim L9415 in a crash also in Co. Donegal, the crew baled out safely. One crewman Flight Sergeant Ricketts had a traumatic time when he was blown out to sea on his parachute. He was stranded on the Collig Rock off Lough Swilly for fourteen hours before he, despairing of rescue, swam the considerable distance to Lenankeel. There Mrs. Kearney revived him from his cold December ordeal, with hot cups of tea and refused to allow the Army to take him until he was ready.

On the same date as T4168 was lost in Donegal, Whitley P5041 from Limavady crashed near Campbeltown in Scotland. P5041 was flown by Flight Lieutenant Billings, and the crew were all killed. Four more aircraft crashed the following month, thankfully without any fatalities; T4223, T4320, T4276 and P5107.

On the 11th of that month P5050 [1] flown by Flying Officer Walker was on a sortie to search for convoy WS6, which was proceeding to Suez via the Cape, when at 16.47 hours in position 56° 30' N 14° 13'W he sighted U93. Using the sun as cover on his starboard beam, he made his run in. At two miles distance the U-boat crashed dived; he reduced height to 50 ft. dropping two depth charges, set to 40 ft. athwart ship. The depth charges dropped at ten to fifteen feet on either side of the hull. The

---

[1] P5050 later crashed of the French coast the crew taken as POW's. This aircraft also survived a crash at Limavady.

aircraft although damaged by returned fire returned safely and landed at Aldergrove.

On March 10th the Squadron operations record book reported that at 20.31 hrs on the 9th March, Whitley P5059 when trying to locate a convoy was fired on by four of the ships from that convoy. The appropriate recognition signals were sent, but the anti aircraft fire persisted and it was not until the aircraft got out of range that the firing stopped. The aircraft was hit in several places; damage was slight but repairable. The aircraft was flown by Pilot Officer Wilkinson and only one of the crew Sergeant Spurgeon was slightly injured.

The following day, T4222 had to ditch at sea at 18.00 hrs following engine trouble. Flying Officer Preston and his crew were eventually picked up uninjured. Another loss occurred on the 13th, when two of Pilot Officer Dears' crew baled out over Galway Bay. Pilot Officer David Midgely landed near Renville pier and swam ashore, Sergeant Robert Harkell landed on Salthill Golf Course. The remaining three crew including Pilot Officer Dear went in with the Whitley; the site in Galway Bay is designated a War Grave.

Crashes continued through-out July and August, the most serious incident being on 23rd August when Z6500 crashed one mile west of the airfield and caught fire. Flying Officer Sproule and Sergeant Naylor were killed as were Pilot Officer Matthews (Navigator), and Sergeant Jones (wireless operator/air gunner). A Lieutenant. Bevan from the destroyer HMS Watchman on board for air experience was also killed. Two of the crew Sergeant Munk and Brawshaw were injured.

On September 15th, several aircraft were on anti submarine sweeps around Convoy O56, when Whitley P5050 flown by Pilot

29

Officer Southan spotted a U-boat at 20.30 hrs in ZNDU 0128. He attacked from 600 ft and the U-boat crash dived immediately. The aircraft released two 500 lb. bombs which fell 20 yards of the U-boat's port bow. No signs of damage were observed and the aircraft set course to warn the convoy. Other aircraft then made further sweeps of the area, but sighted nothing.

On October 2nd Flying Officer Johnston in Whitley 6733 caught a U-boat on the surface in position KDRA 3001 and attacked with two 500 lb. bombs. One was seen to explode approximately 15 yards of the starboard beam of the U-boat; results unknown.

On 22nd October, Pilot Officer Wilkinson in Z6632, sighted a U-boat on the surface at 15.21 hrs, at 52.15oN 16.37oW. The aircraft approached at 30o to the U-boat course on its port quarter, and attacked with two 500 lb. bombs from 600 ft at 120 knots. One explosion was seen 50 yards ahead of the propeller swirl. A second attack was then made from 50 ft on a reciprocal course with two 250 lb. depth charges set at 50 ft, results unknown.

The first U-boat 'kill' using ASV. Mk II radar was attributed to 502 Squadron's Flying Officer Holdsworth, when Whitley Z9190 sank U-206 in the Bay of Biscay on 30 November 1941. The Squadron were the first in Coastal Command to be equipped with ASV. MkII. radar. Flying Officer Holdsworth was not credited with this kill at the time, a first in many ways. A first for ASV. II radar, a first for 502 Squadron and possibly a first for Limavady and Northern Ireland.

Z9190 contacted U206, commanded by Kapitänleutnant Herbert Opitz, at five miles on ASV. They sighted the U-boat at three miles, which, on sighting the aircraft, crashed dived. As the submarine was fully submerged when the Whitley arrived, Flying

Officer Holdsworth estimated its position and released a stick of three depth charges. The water turned a dirty brown colour. Holdsworth then flew along the U-boats probable track and released another stick of three depth charges. Although they hung around for thirty two minutes nothing more was seen.

It is possible Whitley Z9190 had moved to Chivnor and took off from there when it carried out this attack, however records show Z9190 involved in an accident at Limavady on December 9th. of that year, nine days after the attack.

The 'kill' was only confirmed from post war research. Flying Officer Holdsworth was not around to take credit as he was unfortunately killed on 4th March the following year. He had transferred to Coastal Command Development Unit at Ballykelly. He died when the Beaufort AW271 they were in crashed. A parachute had not released properly during tests and the aircraft lost control. It crashed behind the Rectory in Ballykelly. Flying Officer Holdsworth is buried in Oxford Cemetery.

On December 1st Whitley 9124 took off on an anti-submarine sweep at 06.51 hrs. At 11.48 hrs the aircraft, piloted by Pilot Officer Cave attacked a U-boat in position 47.00oN 11.35oW on a course of 255 Deg and making five knots. The aircraft sighted the boat on the surface when flying at a height of 4,500 ft and at a distance of two miles while flying on a bearing of 045o. Pilot Officer Cave closed throttles and dived from out of the sun to 1,000 ft when it turned 90o to starboard. When the aircraft was at 50 ft and about 100 yds. distance on reciprocal track of the U-boat, six depth charges were released in one stick. Three bursts were seen forward of the U-boat, one right on bows, one on port amidships and one on starboard quarter. The aircraft rear gunner saw the U-boat covered completely by upheaval of water for

Wings Over The Foyle

about five seconds. The aircraft then made one and three quarters circles attacking the U-boat on a track of 360o with machine gun fire from both front and rear turrets. Five similar attacks were made. Pilot Officer Caves landed back at Limavady at 16.38 hrs. He was later awarded the DFC; he was killed while at Ballykelly in May 1943.

Air-crew from 502 (Ulster) Squadron taken before the War and the move to Limavady. From left to right Flying Officer Garrett, Pilot Officer Harrison, Flight Lieutenant Corry, Flying Officer Pinfold, Flight Lieutenant Gleave, Pilot Officer Bell and Pilot Officer Hunter McGiffin, kneeling.(Photo H McGiffin).

Wings Over The Foyle

Left; Flight Lieutenant Dickson who left 502 Squadron Limavady after his crash on Loughermore, he later returned to Ballykelly and did two tours on B24 Liberators. He is now retired and living in Belfast
Right; Wing Commander Hunter McGiffin, he transferred out of 502 Squadron and Limavady early in the war, after being a flight instructor he commanded a station in the Cotswolds, before the end of the war he transferred back to Bishop's Court, N. Ireland. He is now retired in Crawfordsburn.

No.221 Squadron and the story of Wellington W5653.

The Squadron.

In 1940, with the situation in the North Atlantic at a very critical stage, U Boats were going through their 'happy times' against Britain's Merchant Shipping, ensuring a casualty rate of frightening proportions.

In these early days of what was to become known as 'The Battle of the Atlantic', the co-operation between the RAF Coastal Command and the Royal Navy, which eventually ensured success, had not yet developed. However, squadrons of Hudsons and Wellingtons bombers were training in efforts to rapidly expand Coastal Command. Their job was to engage in anti-submarine patrols and provide invaluable air cover in the Western Approaches.

One such Wellington squadron was No.221 Squadron, formed at Bircham Newton in Norfolk England. On 21 November 1940, it began a period of training under the command of Wing Commander Tim Vickers and Pilot Officer Parr as Squadron Adjutant. The air-crew came from various units. 500 and 608 Squadrons had instructions to send what amounted to around 20 pilots and wireless operators, mainly auxiliaries who had become fed up with tedious uneventful east coast convoy patrols in Anson and Botha aircraft.

Some Navigators were posted from Blenheim squadrons with a good deal of flying experience but none had any long range over-sea navigation behind them. Others such as Flight Officer

Bannerman, the Squadron Gunnery Leader, came from No. 10 (R.A.A.F) Squadron.

The newly opened satellite airfield at Langham was used for night flying training with a few Wellingtons received from ex-Bomber Training Units. These aircraft were in a very poor condition. By March 1941 new Air to Surface Vessel (ASV) radar equipped Wellingtons started to arrive at Bircham Newton, Norfolk, but not before a number of dawn patrols were carried out in the older aircraft along the Dutch coast with various targets of opportunity being attacked.

The order was given on the 1st March 1941 for the squadrons 'B' flight to transfer to Limavady in Northern Ireland, consisting of the most experienced pilots and the latest aircraft with ASV. equipment. 'A' flight remained at Bircham Newton to continue to train individual crew members to go across to 'B' flight as complete crews.

The first members of 'B' flight flew over to Limavady under the command of Squadron Leader Ian Brolly, a former flying boat pilot and commenced Atlantic patrols in the same month when the U-boats first 'happy time' came to an end. The establishment of a Western Approaches Command Centre in Derby House Liverpool, new convoy escorts and an intensification of patrols by Coastal Command marked a significant turning point.

In the same month, U-boat Command lost three vessels all skippered by 'aces', including Gunther Prien, the hero of Scapa Flow. On 17 March Schepke in U100 and Otto Kretschmer in U99, were sunk by British destroyers H.M.S. Walker and Vanoc. Otto Kretschmer was taken prisoner of war.

Wings Over The Foyle

Limavady Airfield was still being built when 221 arrived to join 502 Squadron. On the airfield only the runways and perimeter track had been finished, work had not yet begun on the technical buildings. Temporary wooden huts were used for flying control and operations room offices, one of which was Station H.Q.- home to the station commander, Group Captain Freddy Pearce. A bare dispersal area was allotted to the squadron, in the middle of which was a small farmhouse and out-buildings. The farmhouse became the flight offices and crew rooms.

Operating under such conditions was difficult. Boggy ground bounded the perimeter track and could not support the weight of an aircraft, so taxiing was a problem. Mud was everywhere. The runways were only 1,200 yards long which left little room for error, close co-operation with flying control and good local knowledge was essential.

Wings Over The Foyle

Top Eric Starling attacking a U-boat in Sept.41 (Ph E Starling)

Bottom Flight Lieutenant Eric Starling and Flying Officer Edwards after their return to Iceland following their successful attack.(Photo E Starling)

No221 Squadron Air-crew; 'Seek and Strike'

The move to Limavady, including Squadron Head Quarters, from Bircham Newton was accomplished by 22 May 1941 when 'A' flight completed final individual training. Even before the squadron had settled in, a set back occurred within 'B' flight. On April 11th. it lost a full crew, when Wellington Bomber, serial no. W5653 - Flight Officer Cattley and Pilot Officer Montague and four crew members crashed into the Urris Mountains in North Donegal at 15.00hrs, on return from an anti-submarine patrol.

To add to the loss of Flying Officer Cattley's crew, another Wellington W5651 with Flying Officer Jimmy Robinson and crew were lost in a crash into Lough Foyle, shortly after taking off on the night of 12 May 1941. It is believed that they ran into a line squall, lost control of the heavily loaded aircraft which crashed and exploded two miles south west of Magilligan Point. However despite these two losses, sporadic sightings of U-boats were made and morale was lifted. By the end of its tour 221 Squadron would have achieved the lowest accident rate, per thousand hours flying, of Coastal Command, thanks in part to having a number of experienced former commercial pilots who were made Captains of aircraft.

The Squadron, despite a high level of operational flying, still managed to put in a lot of training including the 'first' trial with the Leigh Light. These extremely bright searchlights, the invention of Squadron Leader de Verde Leigh, were used to illuminate the U-boat at night from about three quarters of a mile, after the aircraft homed in using ASV. radar. Flying Officer Bliss

Wings Over The Foyle

(Blisso) and crew assigned for this task were eventually absorbed into the Coastal Command Development Unit.

Pilot Officer Hunter McGiffin, from 502 Squadron, vaguely remembers a brief stay of a Wellington fitted with a light driven by an inboard engine carrying out experiments at the airfield. That system was dropped as the engine vibrated the aircraft so much that it was in danger of shaking it apart. He also believes Squadron Leader de Verde Leigh was on site at the time.

Two other crews from 221, those of Flying Officer Jimmy Procter and Flying Officer Jimmy Ray were selected to join the new 120 Squadron. It was being formed up and equipped with Liberators at Nutt's Corner in June 1941, under the command of Belfast man Wing Commander 'mac' McBratney. This new squadron had in its ranks another Belfast man, Terry Bulloch, destined to become Coastal Command's top U-boat killer. Unfortunately Flying Officers Ray and his crew were killed while training in Scotland. Flying Officer Procter later rejoined 221 Squadron in the Western Desert as a member of a Liberator detachment.

The same month 'A flight' was detached to St. Eval in Cornwall where sorties were underway to intercept U-boats returning to their Bay of Biscay bases. Success grew here for the Squadron and quite a number of sightings and attacks were made.

Unfortunately three aircraft were lost, one in air combat; Flying Officer Sanderson was shot down south of the Scilly Isles 11 July 1941, Flying Officer Cakebread failed to return and Pilot Officer Johnson failed to return to Limavady.

Wings Over The Foyle

Crew replacement and training continued at Limavady, where the building programme increased, creating better conditions for crews and operations.

A Wellington training unit was formed at Silloth in July 1941 and 221 Squadron sent Pilot Officer Jack Hoskins, a former 500 Squadron Sergeant Pilot and later Wing Commander, to the new unit to act as senior Instructor.

In each of the months of June July and August the Squadron put in one thousand hours of flying on operations and two hundred and fifty hours on training; over ninety sorties were flown in July alone. It was the highest in the Command.

In August several detachments were sent to Reykjavik in Iceland. In one combined sweep that month by 502 from Limavady and 221 from Reykjavik, three U-boats were attacked

As with the Leigh Light, it was 221 that carried out the first trial of blind bombing radar with automatic release equipment. The crew involved were absorbed into the Command Development Unit. Unfortunately they were lost over the Dutch coast the first patrol the equipment was tried out operationally.

Soon after there was a change at the top when Wing Commander Murdock, RAAF replaced Wing Commander Vickers, who was ordered back to Signals Specialist duties.

A flurry of air and sea activity commenced when the German battleship Bismarck broke out of port. After the sinking of the Hood the orders were given to 'sink the Bismarck'. Six aircraft 'volunteered', from 221 Squadron Limavady to be sent to St. Eval in Cornwall to cover that area in case the Bismarck should make for France. Tony Spooner was told he was one of these 'volunteers'. The Wellington's were equipped with special 500 pound armour piercing bombs, and put on instant readiness in case the Bismarck should be located. Although the excitement was great with air crew listening to every news broadcast, there was trepidation. The battleship was very highly armed and the Wimpys were slow and if the range was too great to return, the orders were to ditch close to a naval unit taking part in the chase and get picked up. The air-crew didn't rate the chances of their success very highly, against such a heavily armed ship, but they were not invited to reason why. In the event, after the Bismarck was found by a Catalina from Lough Erne, it was crippled by the 'stringbags' of the Fleet Air Arm. No one drank to the health and bravery of these Swordfish crews, with more sincerity than did Tony Spooner and crews of 221 Squadron.

The Squadron were told they were to be moved to Reykjavik and at the same time three crews were to be posted to Malta for night reconnaissance duties, their ASV was the first airborne radar on the island. Flight Lieutenant Milton, Flying Officer Watson and Flying Officer Spooner (later to become Squadron Leader, DSO, DFC) were selected. No.221 Squadron, had in its short nine month of existence, established itself as a hard working efficient squadron. It had attacked sixteen U-boats, which was in those early days, an excellent record.

The Squadron wanted to stay at Limavady as they had settled in, and where the aircraft maintenance was being carried out in a newly built hanger which had been allocated to them. Their plan was to stay at Limavady and send a detachment to Iceland, this was rejected. However they were allowed to retain the aircraft servicing facility at Limavady. No 221 Squadron left their mark on Limavady aerodrome's history during their five month stay.

Wings Over The Foyle

The Squadron left for Iceland in September where, soon after the move they got their first confirmed 'kill'. Eric Starling caught and bombed a submerging U-boat, which he photographed with his own camera. The Squadron would stay at Limavady and Iceland until December 1941, when it returned to Bircham Newton to prepare for a move to the Middle East via Malta.

Wings Over The Foyle

Top, A 221 Squadron Wellington DF-S which forced landed on the coast of France near Brest, in the background a sunken U-boat supply ship. The Wellington crew were picked up by the Destroyer *Kappel* out of Derry

Bottom, Walter Zigmond and crew 221 Squadron on detachment from Limavady to St. Eval

43

Wings Over The Foyle

Crash Site Of Wellington W5653

The Story Of Wellington W5653.

Wellington W5653 took off from Limavady at 05.55hrs 'a Good Friday' on what was scheduled as a convoy escort patrol. The aircraft would have set a course for the island of Innistrahul and then turned west at Malin Head and out into the Atlantic. Its sortie completed, the aircraft on its return to base that afternoon encountered heavy mist. W5653 reportedly over flew Limavady at 14.35hrs, possibly guided by Q.D.M.(see page 63) but was unable to sight the airfield. Lost and south west of the airfield the aircraft flew over Lough Swilly. Unaware of the danger and unfamiliar with the local terrain they crashed into the Urris Hills. They hit the hills at 1,200ft, above Dunree Head, killing all six crew instantly.

The Urris Hills rise 1,300ft from the Swilly, sweep into steep rock-enclave mountain slopes and form over into the Gap of Mamore. Two detachments of Irish soldiers, one from Fort Dunree on the left and the other from Fort Lenan, on the right, began a search of the Urris Hills. The former Officer in charge of the Dunree detachment told me,

" I ordered my men to link hands on the way up the mountain because the mist was so thick. A rifle shot was to be the signal that the aircraft had been located."

It was the Lenan detachment who found the wreckage first, Matt Kemmy and Hugh Queike being the first two men on the scene. I spoke to both men in late March 1990 and they indicated that the wreckage lay in two areas but close to each other. Matt saw one of the crew apparently sitting against a rock. This surprised him, given the state of the wreckage and he thought to himself for a

Wings Over The Foyle

moment, that at least one of the crew survived. However on getting closer he realised that he, like his five other crew members, was very dead. Given the angle and speed of around 160 mph of impact it was hardly a surprise.

The force of the impact resulting in fire and devastation, made a lasting impression on Hugh. He admitted it took him a few weeks to shake off the shock of the experience.

It was not until the following evening that the six bodies were brought down the mountain, into the little village of Lenankeel. They were laid out in the local forge, before being moved again to the blockhouse at Fort Dunree.

The usual arrangements were put into effect and the bodies were handed over at Bridgend back into UK territory with full military honours. Photographs of the hand-over were taken at the time, and these are to be seen in the tourist audio/visual display at Fort Dunree.

Wings Over The Foyle

Flying Officer Alfred Patrick Cattley - RAF

History.

Alfred Cattley was born in Petrograd, Russia in 1916, he was the son of Patrick Oswald Cattley and the great grandson of James Richard Cattley of York who had gone to Russia in 1841 as an English Merchant to trade between Russia and the UK.

In the year following Alfred's birth the Russian revolution started which resulted in all the Cattleys having to scramble back to the UK with just a few possessions to their name. Alfred's father seemed to have set up home in Ealing, West London close to other family members who themselves just got out of Russia in time.

Education:-

Little is known about his early years but at the age of 14 he was sent to Berkhamsted School where he passed his School Certificate examinations and served in the Cadet Force there. He sat a further commercial exam in 1935 whilst employed as a junior accountant in the City of London.

Military history:-

Alfred joined the Territorial Army in 1936 in the Artists Rifles but was discharged in 1938 when he was accepted into the Auxiliary RAF on a short service commission of four years for pilot training. He was posted to the Central Flying School at Ansty (Coventry) which was operated by a civil company, Air Training Services Ltd.

Having passed his basic training, he spent the remainder of 1938 and early 1939 at No.8 Flying Training School (RAF) at Montrose in Scotland, having been awarded his flying badge in October 1938. Alfred passed out with 70.2% marks and was listed as an 'average pilot'.

Now a Pilot Officer, he was posted to No.1 Coastal Artillery Co-Operation Unit at Gosport, flying Ansons in March 1939 and spent 12 months there before being posted to NO.608 Sqn Coastal Command based at Thornaby again flying Ansons but now on the East Coast convoy patrols. He was promoted to Flying Officer in September 1940. In December 1940, he was posted to the newly forming 221 Sqn based at Bircham Newton in Norfolk.

Conversion to Wellington aircraft seems to have been carried out at Bircham Newton. January to March 1941 was a working up period on Wellingtons using ex Bomber Command aircraft. The Squadron split into A and B flights with the more experienced pilots going to B flight, whilst A flight continued on conversions and night flying. B flight, waiting for their new operational aircraft to arrive (equipped with then the most secret Mk 2 ASV. radar) started limited offensive EMRO patrols over the North Sea with dawn patrols over the Dutch Coast.

It had been decided that when the first six operational aircraft reached 221 and allotted to B flight, that they would transfer to Limavady in N. Ireland which was to be their new base, and there to commence offensive patrols over the Western Approaches searching for U-boats. Alfred was allocated to one of these new aircraft, serial No. W5653 and was one of the first three pilots and crew to transfer to Limavady.

Wings Over The Foyle

Flying Officer Alfred Cattley RAF.

Wings Over The Foyle

Top; right and left, Sergeant Bateman

Bottom; Sergeant Badman

Pilot Officer James Montague - RAFVR

Pilot Officer James Montague RAFVR was buried in Beconsfield Cemetery, Bucks, grave 93. He was aged 24.

Sergeant (obs) John Bateman RAFVR

Sergeant John Bateman RAFVR, was buried in St. Matthew's Church, Stonebridge Links, section Q , grave 44.

Sergeant Wireless Operator Air Gunner F.K. Whalley - RAFVR

Sergeant F.K. Whalley, Wireless Operator, Aircraft Gunner, RAFV was buried at Whitenash Road cemetery, Leamington, section 109, grave 220. He was aged 19.

Sergeant Wireless Operator Air Gunner Frederick Neill - RAFVR

Frederick George Neill was the only son of Hugh and Mary Neill and was born in West Hartlepool, Co. Durham in 1919. His father was head chauffeur to Mr. William Ropner, head of a family shipping company with offices in Darlington.

Fred Neill, as he was known by his family, attended school in West Hartlepool and on leaving took a two year course in secretarial studies at the school of commerce in West Hartlepool, after which he was employed by the South Durham Steel and Iron Company Limited. Writing short stories, some of which were accepted, and supporting Hartlepool United football team were Fred's hobbies.

Fred's father Hugh came from Ireland, most probably Ulster, and his mother's family from the Whitby area of North Yorkshire

The family moved often between the Ropner estate and summer home near Bedale Yorkshire and the Ropner winter home in West Hartlepool. The children Fred and Nancy stayed in West Hartlepool when they got older as Fred was working and Nancy attending high school. At the outbreak of war the Ropners moved to their estate in west Yorkshire for the duration and it was here Fred's parents where when Fred was killed. His body was taken to Yorkshire.

FRED NEILL

Sergeant Frederick Neill RAFVR is buried in St. Gregory's Church yard, Bedale, Yorks. He was aged 22.

Sergeant Wireless Operator Air Gunner Brinley Badman - RAFVR

Sergeant Brinley Badman RAFVR is buried in Wesley Methodist Churchyard, Varteg, Pontypool, Monmouthshire on the south side of the church.

Top Sergeant Whalley's grave

Bottom right; Sergeant Neill's grave Bedale Yorks.

Bottom left, Sergeant Fred Neill.

Wings Over The Foyle

What Happened On The Night Of 11 April 1941?

As there were no survivors, we have been left to gather all available information on the flight, and the subsequent crash from records and the experiences of others, to come to our final conclusions. We draw on the invaluable experience of two former 221 squadron pilots of note, Tony Spooner and Eric Starling, who were at Limavady in these early days as Flying Officers.

Tony Spooner's Proposition:-

'As to what caused the fatal accident. It <u>was</u> difficult to navigate with poorly trained navigators, and many Wellington crews became hopelessly lost over the Atlantic without landmarks and with no Met stations for accurate forecasts of wind. The Air to Surface Vessel(ASV.) was crude and difficult to interpret accurately. It required almost a sixth sense and some never attained this. Limavady had no efficient let down through cloud procedure which is why Eric Starling and I (and others) had to invent one using the ASV. ground trainer. We were in effect ,a hastily assembled crew flying an aircraft not designed for our work and using an early form of experimental aid (ASV.) about which we had been told almost nothing. The miracle is that so few others came to grief in that difficult terrain.

My guess regarding the loss of W5653, presuming that she overflew Limavady at 14.35 above cloud base ,is; after over-flying Limavady the pilot was directed back using QDM's and carried on in a NW direction hoping for a glimpse of the sea (it was broad daylight) through a gap in the cloud. Finding none, they reversed course and guided by QDM's again flew towards Limavady in hope. Almost at once a crew member reported 'we

Wings Over The Foyle

have just passed over a lough'. Skipper weighs up the situation; 'it can't be Lough Foyle, we passed over Limavady 15 mins. ago, so it was probably Lough Swilly...say we'll carry on a bit and come a bit lower when we see the next lough; that will be Lough Foyle again. We can then drop down over it and approach to land visually.

However the first lough sighted in a cloud gap might not have been Lough Swilly but the small lough to the west terminating at Milford [Mulroy Bay]. To a co-pilot sitting on the right of an aircraft, that small lough could have seemed long enough to be Lough Swilly. In the end, when a second lough appeared and it might have been taken to be Lough Foyle,..the aircraft drops down...!'

Tony Spooner also indicates that he used to attempt to make either a visual or an ASV. contact with Tory Island first, and then creep down in bad weather over the sea, pick up Malin Head and Inishtrahul by visual and skirt round into the narrow entrance of the lough.

It is also worth mentioning, in relation to over flying Irish Airspace, Tony Spooner indicates that he supposes that there must have been instructions / orders in relation to the this. He knew there was an air corridor over Eire to the flying boat base at Lough Erne, along which RAF aircraft were allowed to fly. However, as there was no AA and no fighters, they were not bothered about infringing Irish airspace, especially in bad weather conditions such as on the 11 April 1941. Thus he thinks it quite probable that W5653 flew over Donegal on its way out to the NW having overshot base.

Tony Spooner quotes an incident which happened to him while at Limavady, which perhaps illustrates how Alfred and his crew might better have handled things on the 11 April. Tony got lost one especially foul night when cloud cover reduced ASV radar efficiency to almost zero (as a navigation aid) .Fifteen minutes after the Irish coast should have appeared, they could still only see water under them, so rather than blunder on blindly, he got his 2nd pilot to fly a square search pattern to hold position while he and his Sergeant Observer both checked their navigational plots. Obviously still unsure of their location, Tony then climbed up through the cloud for better radio reception and instructed the wireless operator to open up the set and get whatever bearings he could, from anywhere. It took them a full 30 minutes on the radio to get sufficiently good bearings to work out their true approximate position and be able to set a positive course for Limavady.

As Tony comments, he had been experimenting with fuel/boost settings for maximum economy for some time before this particular flight, and was thus very glad on this occasion that he had the reserves necessary for all the extra stooging about trying to get their bearings.

Eric Starlings Version:-

'Inexperienced pilots and navigators do strange things when they are flying blind. I remember, when we were in Iceland (still with 221 Squadron) Squadron Leader Brolly having an argument with his navigator and finishing with, 'The truth of the matter is that we are lost!'.-'Yes I am, so what?' was his unanswerable reply. When they eventually came down they broke cloud flying down a valley with snow clad mountains on either side. I presume their ASV. was not working .Good luck prevented another flight into a mountainside.'

In other correspondence Eric Starling points to some of the problems of the job. The request no air-crew liked, was to extend to their PLU (prudent limit of endurance). This was requested when a replacement aircraft was unavailable for whatever reason. The problem was, if you stayed too long you ran out of fuel and ended in the sea, if on the other hand you got a tail wind on the way home and landed with fuel in your tank you were accused of having LME (low moral fibre).

Pointing to reasons for otherwise unexplainable accidents Eric states *"Why weren't they flying a bit higher?. Pilots fly into mountains because they know exactly where they are when, in fact, they are somewhere else"*. He goes on to tell of an incident which occurred (to him) in this period. *"I very very nearly flew into the St. Kilda cliffs while I was with 221 Coastal Command Wellington Squadron at Limavady, Northern Ireland. St. Kilda was the starting point for an anti submarine search of the Atlantic. The weather that day was exceptionally bad but we were asked to keep below cloud if possible so that we could keep a look out for the crew of an aircraft which had ditched somewhere in the area. I was flying along about 150 feet just below cloud in rain and mist. St. Kilda was visible on the radar and I asked my navigator who was working the radar to keep me just clear of the islands. However a misunderstanding occurred between us, and suddenly, through the mist I saw, straight ahead of me, the shoreline and bottom of the cliffs. I stuck the Wellington on its wingtip and did the quickest turn I have ever done. My comments to the crew were quite unprintable"*.

Wings Over The Foyle

Background To The Crash:-

As Alfred and his crew did not crash due to enemy action, it is worth setting the scene to illustrate as to how accidents such as theirs happened.

At the time in question air crews, in Coastal and Bomber Command, were quite on their own, once aloft. They had almost no support from the ground concerning their position, no radar control and no radio talk back. No IFF equipment for ground controllers to identify them by (such as was given to fighter command) and in this case over the Atlantic with no reliable Met information.

These days it seems difficult to understand.

All navigation and decisions concerning the flight were down to the crew as a whole without the benefit of radio contacts that were of any real use. The only form of contact with the base was by Morse code because the aircraft were not equipped with VHF sets as supplied to fighters.

The only form of 'fix' the radio operator could get with the base was by Morse code, and try to gauge their position from the bearing transmitted back to them. That is, he got a ground station to inform him of the bearing his transmission was coming from. Flying around in either darkness or 100% cloud, he was then expected to be able to set a course back to base.

To an experienced navigator and wireless operator, such vague input may have been sufficient. But in 1941 the RAF Bomber and Coastal Command had been obliged to expand rapidly and air-crew did not have the necessary experience from hasty training to be able to cope.

Wings Over The Foyle

Many similar mistakes were made such as that which befell W5653. The resulting crash into the Urris Hills cannot, nor should not, be attributed to any one member of the crew. It should instead, be laid at the door of the training programs which left new crews insufficiently practised to cope in poor weather conditions.

One good thing came out of crash W5653 and numerous other aircraft lost in similar circumstances, was the introduction of the Beam Approach Beacon System. Something vaguely similar was being tried by members of 221 squadron at Limavady as a 'home brew' invention to give themselves some form of radar guidance for a let down in cloud, and to put them in line with the runway, and indicate its range ahead of the aircraft.

Before explaining this, it is perhaps as well to give some idea as to how the 'new and top secret radar' which was fitted to 221 squadron's Wellingtons worked:- The official terminology used, for what was in reality, airborne radar looking at the sea surface, was: ASV. or Air to Surface Vessel. The plight of the Royal Navy in attempting to protect the Merchant convoys was well understood, they were under strength for the task in hand, and at that time unsupported by the USA (which was still neutral). The German U-boats were taking a ghastly toll on merchant shipping bringing vital war materials into this country.

The rate of sinking far outstripped launchings, it was only a matter of time before our Nation would have been brought to its knees. This the Germans knew well enough and pressed home their attacks.

At that time, the submarine was essentially a surface vessel with a reasonably high surface, but a very low underwater speed Considered vulnerable to aircraft attack, the idea was to assist the

Wings Over The Foyle

Royal Navy by rushing into service, aircraft of Coastal Command equipped with ASV. and depth charges which could both locate subs and bomb them to destruction.

Air to Surface Vessel (ASV.):-

So how did this ASV. work?. One has to remember that at the time 221 Squadron was equipped with the very latest technology, which by comparison to our standards today seems antiquated. In 1941 they WERE in the forefront of the radar war which would eventually help to bring victory for the Allies as the final outcome.

The idea was to use two different transmitters of radar signals, one in the nose and another on the dorsal fuselage surface. The nose antenna sent a radar pulse out which radiated ahead of the aircraft. If there was anything on the seas surface, its reflected signal should have been received by beam antennae slung under both port and starboard wings.

In a similar fashion, radar pulses from the dorsal fuselage antennae radiated out to port and starboard and if any return echo was present, it was received on antennae which were fixed to the vertical sides of the rear fuselage. Any pulses were fed into a cathode ray tube (TV screen) and showed up as a 'blip' or return signal on it.

The operator could switch from ahead to beam search at will.

The theory was fine, but in practice the crews found that the installation was rather insensitive, especially if the sea conditions were rough when their sets got returns from waves which reflected their radar signals, giving false echoes or 'interference'.

Such was the new equipment that Alfred and his fellow Officers went to war with in April 1941 in 221 Squadron. Prototypical and experimental as it was, it laid the foundations of a weapon that would eventually outclass German radar developments and resulted in aiding the destruction of the U-boat as a threat.

The loss of Alfred's crew plus many others whilst stationed at Limavady got the rest of the squadron members thinking as to how they could improve their chances of a safe let-down to the airfield when it was obscured by a cloud, fog or darkness or even both.

By experimenting with the squadrons ASV. trainer (a ground based device) they located antennae to it placed either side of the runway pointing down the approach path of the returning aircraft. They used the returning aircraft onboard ASV. radar to 'trigger' this base transponder, which then emitted a series of pulses from each antenna in turn. The operator in the aircraft received these transmissions on his cathode ray tube which then told him if the aircraft was 'left or right' of the runway. He could then give the pilot course corrections to ensure they were 'flying down the transponder radio beam' which meant they were lined up with the runway.

Range from runway was calculated by observing the signal strength of the base transmissions on the onboard radar set. From local knowledge of the surrounding area, the pilot thus knew what height was necessary at various ranges from the airfield and could control his descent accordingly.

It is interesting to note that this 'Beam Approach System' was successful enough for 221 Squadron. The Telecommunications Research Establishment, a Government Experimental Department who had tested the very ASV. sets that 221 Squadron were using operationally before going into squadron service, following up on their research, produced an improved version which went into general service and doubtless saved many lives.

It is perhaps typical that the original work and ideas for this life saving device invented as it was by colleagues of Alfred Cattley, was never officially recognised by the Air Ministry.

Tony Spooner carried the idea even further forward later in 1941. In Malta his skilful ground radar operator Flying Officer Albert Glazer fitted a transponder onto H.M.S. Aurora, the leading cruiser of Force K, with which the Specials Duties Flight (SDF) was co-operating They were attacking Italian convoys running troops and supplies, at night, to North Africa. Thus the SDF aircraft could pin-point by ASV. receiver where the Royal Navy task force was and direct it onto enemy shipping that the SDF aircraft had found. Again all 'home brew' but highly successful in its operation. A similar arrangement was made in Malta when co-operating with the Swordfish torpedo carrying aircraft of 830 Squadron Fleet Air Arm

Q.D.M.

QDM was a 'Q' code word for asking the airfield base to transmit a signal to the aircraft to assist the crew to obtain a bearing from the airfield in bad visibility when it was not possible to see the ground. It was not a system whereby a navigational 'fix' could be calculated, only a bearing.

The sole object of a QDM call from an aircraft to its base was to receive a QDM bearing which enabled the aircraft to find its way back to the airfield.

It was not the airfield transmitting a signal but the airfield reading the signal from the aircraft and noting from which direction it had come. The airfield then advised the aircraft accordingly.

The wireless operator in the aircraft would note the airfield signal source in the form of a compass bearing and the pilot would turn onto that heading. The wireless operator would continue to monitor the signal source by way of bearing which might for example have gone from 120 deg., 123 deg., 125 deg. and suddenly turn to 307 deg., 300 deg., 295 deg.; indicating a reversal of bearing having passed over or close by the airfield. This was the only form of fix available to the crew from a series of QDM.

From then on it was up to the crew to get back down as best they could.

Contrary to popular misconceptions, the aircraft were not guided down by QDM's at all, as the airfield radio staff operating the radio sets had no means of plotting the incoming aircraft (i.e. no radar!) but were simply putting out a signal on receiving a QDM request. It was up to the air-crew to make the best of the QDM signals that they had asked for.

Regarding W5653, if we believe the Irish Army reports which indicate they were told by the RAF personnel who came down to Dunree to inspect the crash site, W5653 had already over-flown the airfield at 14.35hrs. That is, five minutes after their estimated time of arrival they were in cloud and hidden from the ground. It means that either their dead reckoning was spot on, or, more likely that they were feeling their way in on a series of QDM bearings.

Wings Over The Foyle

If this Irish Army report is correct then it seems logical that they then made a very wide right hand orbit from south via west and north onto an easterly heading and in doing so hit the Urris Hills.

More experienced pilots such as Starling or Spooner say that they would in these circumstances have attempted to keep under the cloud base whilst over sea, and checked a landfall on Tory or Rathlin Islands in order to skirt along the coast, and look for the entrance to Lough Foyle. It is impossible to speculate any further as to why Wellington Bomber W5653 was so high and flying blind in clouds. Are the Irish Army reports correct? We shall never know.

Wings Over The Foyle

On The Site Of W5653

Ground work on this crash site began on 1 October 1989 and continued until 10 December 1989, during which time nine visits were made to the area. Further interviews were carried out in March 1990. If ever a site was evasive to pinpoint it was this one, with no surface items visible and the site lying at about 1,100 - 1,200 feet among rock and heather in a broken up terrain. It was through the help of local man Sean Ferguson that we finally located it.

It was not the highest site I've ever climbed by any means but to date it has certainly been the most troublesome. Despite heavy rain and the short nights, two previous attempts had been made from Lenankeel to locate the site but it was an approach from wrong direction and it not the weather that thwarted us on these two occasions. However, the visits to Lenankeel were far from wasted, two local men told me that after the crash,and for many months afterwards, tinkers had taken advantage of a cliff path (which we used in our first attempts to locate the site) to mule pack wreckage down the hill. I was also told that as children, the men had pushed an engine over the cliff into the sea.

Some items of wreckage, including a fuselage support for the geodetic framework, still remain in the area. The site itself was a small burned area amongst the rocks and an undercarriage leg lay in the heather with several small items of wreckage littered over the site. Several more visits to the crash site were made and on the last Sean was to prove invaluable.

Sean's father, John Ferguson had been one of the soldiers engaged that night in locating the crash. He told me that for some time afterwards, while on duty in the blockhouse at Fort Dunree you could smell a lingering aroma of burnt heather.

Two small poignant pieces were found at the site: a black RAF button and part of a wrist-watch frame.

On our last but one visit to the site, we pushed the undercarriage leg upright into the rocks to act as both a marker and reminder of the crew of Wellington W5653.

The idea of a more classic and traditional memorial to mark where the six air-crew died formed into reality when we decided to make and erect a cross on the site. John Ferguson kindly donated a brass plaque to mount on the cross inscribed with the six names. In May 1991 we again climbed up to the crash site and in our own private way, erected the cross to ensure that here at least were six men who gave their lives; but are no longer members of the forgotten many.

On The Site Of Wellington W5653 - Urris Hills

Research Up-Date

Since erecting the cross in 1991 work continues through desk research, greatly accelerated when through the 221 Sqn association, a cousin of the pilot, Tim Cattley contacted me, seeking information on the crash.

Thus started a further two year period of work on the crash (1992-94), during which time relatives of the crew, with the exception of Sgt. Whalley were traced.

The fruit of that work has now been laid down in print in this publication.

During the summer of 1994, three more visits were made to the crash site, during which time, with the help of John Kearney from

Wings Over The Foyle

Lenankeel, a boss cover and reduction gear wheel were salvaged down the cliff into Lenan.

A new weather resistant plaque has been made for the cross. The cross was removed and re-varnished by Sean Ferguson.

John Quinn and Robert Taylor with former Irish soldier John Ferguson, who was a member of the search party which went to look for W5653

Wings Over The Foyle

Top; A photograph from the crash site of W5653, showing the Collig Rock where F/Sgt. Ricketts swam to safety Dec 1940

Bottom; Forge in Lenan where a plaque is to be erected and dedicated on 9 April 1995

Pilot Training Course.

In 1932 the British Government decided that 'the ten year rule' of non expansion of the RAF should be relaxed because of events developing in Europe. It was quite some time before any form of practical effect came from this decision and it was not until the annual estimate of 1934 authorised an increase in front line squadron strength. This expansion program would have put an impossible strain on the existing pilot training organisation.

It was decided to expand the existing small nucleus of training schools and at the same time change the training format. Rather than have the Squadrons complete the training a new scheme was planned.

Under this scheme it was considered necessary to provide pilots who could assume an immediate operational role when posted to their squadron The revised training course would have a higher initial standard of flying, navigation, night in service aircraft, and weapons air training.

To achieve this higher standard, training was divided into three separate stages:-

- Initial training at a civilian run training school operated on a commercial basis under an air ministry contract. Here the pupil was in civil clothing but under quite strict discipline. He learned to fly solo in light training aircraft and gained a degree of instruction in both instrument and simple cross country flying. This 8 week course was followed by a 2 week course at an RAF Depot where the trainee learned RAF discipline and drill.

Wings Over The Foyle

- An intermediate course of Pilot training at an RAF Service Flying Training School. At the start of this course the trainees were selected for specialisation and split into three sub-groups:- Heavy Bombers /Flying boats and general reconnaissance; Light Bombers and Torpedo: Single and two seat Fighter.
- This course lasted between 13-15 weeks depending on time of year(15 weeks in winter). They flew service trainers, had advanced instruction on instrument flying, simulated night navigation and long cross country flights; they also sat examinations. If the trainee passed all tests he was awarded his flying badge on pass-out.
- An advanced stage course at an RAF Service Flying School were they did advanced blind flying, navigation solely on instruments plus map reading and practical navigation.
- Having completed the three basic stages, trainees were then posted to specialised schools which related to their type selection.
- A number of Initial Flying Training School (Civil) and Flying Training School (RAF) were set up as new establishments across the country. This was supplemented later on by the Empire Air Training Scheme when we were at war and further expansion was necessary to offset operational losses.

Alfred Patrick Cattley. Service No 40888.

How did Alfred slot into the training organisation?

He was at the forefront of the RAF expansion when entering squadron service and was looked upon by RAF Cranwell types as Auxiliary material. This was before war broke out and before the

Wings Over The Foyle

expansion training program got into full swing. Later on when pilot losses mounted, it was accepted that replacement material was 'hostilities only' but sorely needed whatever their method of recruitment.

An indication has been given of the training organisation operation in circa 1938, so that the reader can identify Alfred's training history under the expanded scheme.

After Alfred completed his training he got his first operation posting 608 Squadron at Thornaby on 11 March 1940 exactly 13 months before his last flight.

Their task was to patrol the east coast from Thornby to Leuchars in Scotland in Ansons. Pilot Officer Cattley skippered his first patrol on 6 April 1940 in Anson N 5362. In all he flew seventy nine operation patrols with 608 Squadron and gained promotion to Flying Officer before he received his posting orders to 221 Squadron, then forming at Bircham Newton, on 20 December 1940.

The Squadron trained on ex Bomber Command Mk 1 Wellington while awaiting the new Mk VIII with the latest highly secret ASV. radar. Training was well underway by March when the Squadron were informed by Group that they were to move to Limavady in Northern Ireland. Meanwhile they patrolled the Dutch coast looking for and attacking enemy shipping. The first such patrol was piloted by Flying Officer Spooner on the 3rd March 1940 and the second by Flying Officer Cattley when they bombed Helder quay-side in N Holland.

While the Squadron continued their east coast patrols Wing Commander Tim Vickers flew to Limavady to check on the state of readiness of the airfield. The decision was made to move B flight there just as soon as they received their new operational aircraft.

The 13th March 1941 was an eventful day for Pilot Officer Cattley. On the way back to base, after an attack on a small vessel of the Dutch coast, they lost a prop. The Pegasus engine was prone to seizure. When this happened sometimes, if the crew were lucky, the shaft would shear and the prop spin away from the aircraft. The lose of prop reduced the drag on the Wellington and allowed it to just about stagger along on one engine. This is what happened on this patrol and they were able to make a landing at Bircham Newton, minus a starboard prop. The difficulty with Coastal Command operations was they patrolled at around 600 ft. allowing very little margin for loss of altitude should any such emergency occur.

The next day the first of the new Wellingtons Mk.VIII arrived with ASV. equipment. Over the next six days four more arrived and B Flight stopped patrols in order to concentrate on training on the new aircraft and radar.

By the 29th March A flight had taken over the patrols and B flight began deployment to Limavady to take up its role in protecting the western approaches. Other crises had first to be dealt with. Two of the scheduled five aircraft were diverted to St. Eval in Cornwall to cover a intelligence indication of a possible breakout from the French Atlantic ports of the battle cruisers Sharnhorst and Gneisenau.

On the 2nd April Squadron Leader Brolly and Flying Officer Cattley carried out their first practice flights from Limavady to test the ASV. radar and to get to know the local conditions.

The 3rd April weather conditions at Limavady prevented flying.

Wings Over The Foyle

On the 4th April two convoy escort patrols were flown; the Pilots were Squadron Leader Brolly and Flying Officer Sanderson.[2]

On the 5th April another Atlantic patrol is recorded, flown by Flight Lieutenant Hullock in the sixth Mk VIII Wellington which had been delivered to Limavady five days earlier by Sergeant Smith..

On the 6th April the day the Germans invaded Greece, Flying Officer Cattley flew his first convoy escort patrol from Limavady. The flight was of seven hours duration and landed at 17.45hrs. This was to be his last before the tragic 11th April flight.

On the 11th, the day a famous fortress, Tobruk, was making its name at the start of an eight month siege, Alfred Cattley and his crew of five died at 15.00hrs, crashing into the steep slopes between the old first World War forts of Dunree and Lenan high in the Urris Hills on the West coast of Donegal,. They were unable to locate accurately Limavady aerodrome because of the prevailing weather. Lost and unfamiliar with the terrain, they were flying too low and did not clear the high ground of Croaghcarragh. Now, with the wreckage of Wellington W5653, only a lonely cross stands as a silent sentinel.

---

[2] Flying Officer Sanderson killed on opps 11 July 1941.

The Urris mountain where W5653 crashed; some wreckage still lies on its steep slopes.

Flight Lieutenant Eric Starling, 221 Squadron.

Like Tony Spooner and others at 221 Squadron in 1941, Eric Starling had pre-war civil flying experience, but unlike Tony Spooner who had joined the RAF(VR), he had joined the R.Aux.A.F at the time of Munich in 1938.

Eric Starling was Officer Commanding of 'A' flight, when on 11 October 1941, while flying from Reykjavik in Iceland, he scored the Squadron's first 'kill'.

Flying his Wellington 'H'-Harry('one over the eight', a name he had picked up in the pre-war flying circus days), he and his five crew, Pilot Officer Edwards, Sergeant Woods, Sergeant Dickson, Sergeant Wratton and Flight Sergeant Frusdale, caught the U-boat on the surface.

With Pilot Officer Edwards as Bomb Aimer, he attacked with three 450lb. depth charges set to detonate fifty feet below the surface. They exploded alongside the stern and conning tower. The U-boat was considered sunk by the Navy.

On arrival back at Reykjavik, Eric recalls he did a 'victory' very low pass down the runway. "As we were approaching, my front gunner suddenly remembered the front guns were not on safe. He dashed forward, to lean into the turret and by mistake pressed the wrong button and squirted bullets down the runway!!. I told him that if it produced no comment, I would forget it. Nobody did, so all was well."

Seven months later Eric caught another U-boat on the surface in the Mediterranean. On the 11/12 May 1942, in Wellington Mk VIII Serial B-MD, while on a search for enemy convoys, having

Wings Over The Foyle

already used his bomb load, his log remarks read, "Search for enemy convoy. Sidi Barrani to Sicily and return. Sighted enemy submarine heading for Barrini. Nothing to attack it with. Damm it!."

Eric Starling returned to Limavady and joined 7 OTU when it formed there. He later, as a Squadron Leader, commanded No 304 Ferry Training Unit. The function of this was to prepare crews for ferrying Beaufighters to India and the Middle East. Pilots and wireless operators/ Navigators were crewed up after completing their training, sent to Bristol to collect a new aircraft and then went on to 304 for a fortnight. During this time they were kitted up, the aircraft prepared for the long flight, fuel consumption carefully checked, etc. and the crew sent on long, night and day navigation training, flights over the Atlantic.

Eric Starling continued flying after the war and eventually retired as a British European Airways Captain.

As the Air-crew Remember It.

The young RAF air and ground crew and their families posted to Limavady in the war years, often came to Northern Ireland with mixed expectations. Some came expecting to be billeted in thatch cottages with half doors and chickens nesting in the kitchen; others expected IRA around each corner. In effect some got a pleasant surprise when they found an area outside the practical range of the majority of German bombers and an area which was practically self sufficient in some foods. Here they could enjoy luxuries London had been starved of for months

Anne Spooner, on a short break to visit her husband a Pilot Officer with 221, from her job as an ambulance driver in London, remembers the 'ambrosial food'. She spent a brief time in the hospital in Limavady and had her appendix removed. She actually got poached salmon and - luxury upon luxury - strawberries and thick cream!. For someone from a beleaguered capitol living on dried eggs and spam and working seventy two hours a week, this provided a life time memory.

The other abiding memory was the hospital matron, running the hospital without modern bureaucracy, doing the work herself when necessary, ruling strictly but with 'great good humour and ensuring a high standard of nursing care'.

The social scene at Limavady stepped up a pace in the war years with the two picture houses in competition and getting the best films. There was a dance every night either in the Townhall, the Orange hall or St. Pats. The bars too did a good trade, but as closing time was nine o'clock most of the trade was through the back door. Tony Spooner was highly amused, when in an after hours drinking session, he had to listen to the senior police officer complaining because his wife was the only person in the whole town who actually had to use her ration coupons to buy meat. The Alexander Arms Hotel was the most popular pub for the airmen and it was chock-a-block long after the official closing time of 9 o'clock. The fact that pubs opened all day and a blind eye was turned to the night closing was strange to their English upbringing - but they soon adapted.

The airmen were also in the habit of utilising empty whisky bottles to carry out beer from the mess at Drenagh, to finish at their rooms at Grants farm. Mrs. Grant was appalled one mornings, from the evidence of empty whisky bottles, to think they drank so much and still went flying. "Just six of them--- and eight whole bottles of the hard stuff".

Squadron Leader Spooner also remembers, what to an Englishman was an unusual practice, when the Grants hired a servant girl for six months. She charmed them all with her hard work, honesty and good looks; they often wonder what become of her.

The catering arrangements are also fondly recalled. Mrs. Grant always had a huge pot of potatoes boiling in their skins on the large kitchen range, to which everyone helped themselves, what ever else they wanted they made themselves.

Transport for the Spooners was by a old Ford 8 which Tony had bought for £5 from Flying Officer Jimmy Robinson (see page 38). The car burned as much oil as petrol, the petrol supplied unofficially by the government and appearing magically in the tank when Pilot Officer Spooner was flying on operations. The Ford served them well, with a new engine it lasted until 1946 and they sold it at a profit.

Wings Over The Foyle

Tony Spooner came back to Limavady airfield in 1942/43 as an instructor with 7 OTU. This time he stayed with a bank manager named Irwin who lived a couple miles out of town. The manager had led an eventful life and kept the service people staying with him entertained with his stories.(He had an army officer and his wife as well as the Spooners) Many a pleasant evening was spent on rubbers of bridge in the warmest room in the house, the Irwins lounge. Or they would have been rubbers of bridge if the story telling had stopped long enough to finish them. One story sticks in Tony Spooners mind, when Mr. Irwin was asked if he had ever, in his long banking career, all over Ireland,been held up by 'Republicans'. He replied in that indeed he had, but he continued

"I also asked for a receipt when giving them the money"

"Receipt?" from the incredulous Tony Spooner.

"Yes indeed. The receipt said they had taken £ xyz but it would be returned when they had come into power."

A brief pause as his guests tried to comprehend.

"Otherwise" mused Irwin "it would have been a bit like stealing, wouldn't it".

In outrage Spooner asked, did he not have a gun to protect the banks money.

Irwin replied

"Indeed I did but I didn't like to give them that as a well; -unless- they asked for it."

The local sport of fishing was also adopted by many of the soldiers but Tony recalls the equipment used was rather unconventional, they used mills bombs!. But it didn't effect the taste of the fish, he remembers they were very eatable.

Wings Over The Foyle

As it is for many, the memories of the war for the Spooners was often about food and the availability, or not, of it. And it was this aspect which very often was the catalyst for social meetings between the locals and the service people. The relatively plentiful supply of eggs in Northern Ireland compared to the cities in England, was one such interface; as long as you had a friendly farmer. On one such visit the Spooners, while waiting for the farmers daughter returning with the eggs, were discussing the farmers family who's photographs adorned the walls of the room, they had emigrated to all corners of the world. They enquired of the man if he himself had done any travelling , he scratched his head and tried to remember.

"O yes" he replied "I've been to Derry a couple of times".

But life is about trade and war did not get in the way. As a matter of fact Limavady and Drenagh estate in particular were leading the way. The butter smuggled across to Magilligan from Greencastle was not the only import to the area.

Britain occupied Iceland to utilise its position in the Atlantic and 221 Squadron were moved there but kept their facilities in Limavady, to service the Wellingtons. The critical shortage of vegetables in Iceland and the plentiful supply of ladies stockings and cigarettes there which were rationed here, led to a natural trade of Limavady vegetables for cigarettes, flown out and in courtesy of the RAF.

The wartime poverty of some of the more remote country people sometimes shocked the visitors, particularly in some of the more inaccessible houses, people which normal visitors would never see. The war dragged everyone in, all resources were required and it seemed every corner of Northern Ireland was held up to scrutiny. One such incident concerned an air gunner who missed

Wings Over The Foyle

the last bus back from Coleraine and set out to walk the dozen or so miles back to Aghanloo, on an unpleasant wet and windy night. After some miles in the wet his enthusiasm for the walk waning he saw a small house and thinking he might spend some time in dryer conditions, he knocked the door. He got no reply so venturing in he found the occupants snoring loudly, fast asleep, fully clothed. Their beds were packing cases.

One other indicator of the Limavady life style which gave the Spooners many hours of speculation was the second hand cupboard they acquired to help furnish their rooms when with the Irwins.

Tony Spooner takes up the story

"The cupboard had its own story to tell. Inside the door I found in a clear round copper plate, pencilled the details of the clothes which a previous owner had, many years before, bought. It covered a period of about ten years.

The cupboard had been in the bedroom of three girls and a boy, all very poor farming children. For a year or so all it records was 'James bought boots, Kate bought boots, Sheila bought boots, Mary bought boots. Then the three girls all bought dresses about the time James purchases cease. Then it goes back to the monotony of the girls buying boots. Later first one then the other girls purchases cease at the time when all remaining again bought dresses until finally and rather sadly -and in a less formed handwriting , poor backward Mary is all alone buying annually or biannually, just boots.

It puzzled me for a while until I realised the significance of the new dresses which always coincide with the removal of a child's name!. Then it came to me; one by one the children had left to get married and the dresses- their only new clothes for about ten years, must have been for the wedding. Poor Mary left all alone on the shelf."

Tony Spooner had two spells in Limavady the first as a junior flyer in 221 Squadron, the second as a Squadron Leader Instructor with 7 OTU. When he returned in this role it was to pass on his experience of operational flying to the young pilots in the Operation Training Unit. He reminisces of these visits, "In those often bad weather conditions it was asking a lot of too-hastily trained war time pilots to operate from a marginally small airfield encompassed as it was to the NE and SE by hills. At night for pilots who had scarcely been trained at all to fly by instruments alone, it was asking too much."

Rod Pike, a Warrent Officer Navigator with 221 Squadron, came to Limavady in April 1941 and he like the rest of the Squadron were housed to the east of the airfield. The huts were next to a farmhouse, where the crews could get milk and scones.. One sortie, from Limavady, gave Rod great satisfaction. On the 12 June 1941, U-552 torpedoed and sank the 8,593 ton cargo liner S.S.Chinese Prince, one of three ships sunk by U-boats on that day. The Wellington's of 221 were sent to look for survivors. Rod's aircraft found them and were able to direct navy destroyers to pick them up. Rod was fond of Limavady and was pleased to be posted, later in the war, to Ballykelly with 59 Squadron, where they were involved in the sinking of a U-boat.

Wings Over The Foyle

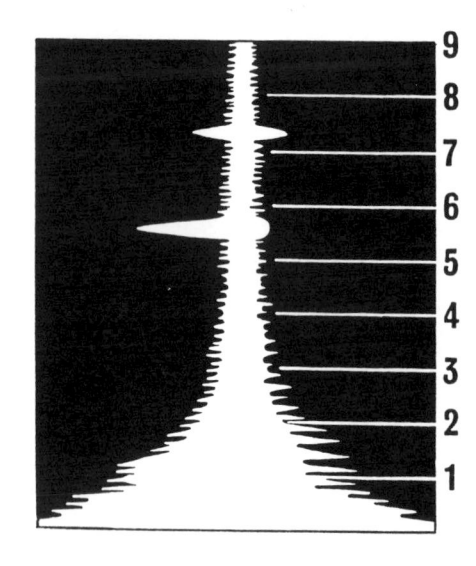

Top Left; Tony Spooner.

Top Right; An ASV screen as seen by WWII air-crew.

Bottom; Ex 221 Squadron crews transferred to Ballykelly CCDU.

84

Wings Over The Foyle

Top; Gorteen House once the Sergeant's Mess for 502 Squadron
Bottom; Drenagh House, the Officers Mess in the early days.

Wings Over The Foyle

Local stories

Limavady was a Wellington base but early squadrons flew Whitleys. The Whitleys were a improvised stopgap until more suitable aircraft could be supplied. Jimmy McLaughlin of Greencastle from his vantage point in the Donegal Hills remembers them as slow droning aircraft as they flew down the Lough. Although the Limavady Squadron were the first to be fitted with the Mk. II ASV. their lack of range and speed mitigated to produce a less than suitable aircraft but a useful one none the less.

The need to patrol the North Atlantic was so great that operations were started from Limavady before construction was complete. The early military personnel camped in tents, one group of Royal Engineers had to shift sites quickly when they camped too close to the old pig farms, which were so extensive in Artikelly, the pig lice 'ate them alive'. The soldiers had to be fumigated to get rid of the pests and were given a wide berth for a time by the locals. Later personnel from 617 Royal Engineers, under Lieutenant Morrisey, who had just been evacuated from Dunkirk helped complete the runways

The building contractors, Stewart and Partner, worked seven days a week to complete the work. They paid a tradesman £5 15/6p per seven day week, a further five shillings was deducted for war savings. Local people were in full employment building and providing services. Tommy Huston remembers running a water main from the main pipe at the Aghanloo Orange Hall and setting up groups of stand-pipes for the airmen to use. Tommy worked through the war years fitting and plumbing in the airfield. On one occasion a guard thinking he was acting suspiciously arrested him at bayonet point. The Station Commander Group Captain Turner had some sharp words for the guard; he was amazed that anyone didn't know *Tommy Huston*. Group Captain Turner later came back to Limavady to spend his last years in retirement in the area he grew to love. During the War years he had lived in Limavady in Rittters house opposite the Court House in Main Street.

The farms in the immediate airfield area were requisitioned by the Government after Munich, and around the sites Nissan huts and wooden huts were built as temporary accommodation. No. 221 Wellington Squadron took over a farmhouse in a dispersal area. Some of Cochrane's two farms and Moor's farm land was also taken(now Witherows) and many other houses knocked down to make way for the runways. There were houses which were used for accommodation early in the war which were demolished later. One such was the house of a Miss Maginnis. A lot of the larger houses in the area 'put up' airmen.Drenagh had some of the senior officers and had Nissan Huts in the grounds, it was also an officers mess. Gorteen House was the sergeant's mess for 502 Squadron, then the property of a Captain Canard. Bolea house also had officers billeted, one of which got into trouble, when despite a request for assistance from a rescue party he did not help when Wellington HF838 from 7 OTU crashed into the Curley Burn just below the house. Five crew died.

The RAF had people 'put up' in all the larger houses for miles around as quite a few early flyers were in established careers and had wives who moved with them. The memories of the acquaintances and friendships made have lasted through the years. One poignant memory for the Grants of Derrybeg was that of an flyer named Bancroft. He was posted to Limavady in March of 1941. After a month he got leave and was married, he and his

Wings Over The Foyle

bride came back and stayed with the Grants until he was again posted in August, by the time they moved his wife was pregnant. But he didn't live to see his son. His wife treasured their happy but all too short month together in Derrybeg and named her boy Derry. After the war they came to visit the area so that her son could see their brief family home.

Many other airmen left their mark. Ian Grant clearly remembers a young 502 Squadron airman called Bill Caves who, with his wife, stayed with them. One reason Ian remembers Bill was that one of the senior officer had expressed his concern to Ian's father as to level of training Bill Cave had obtained. They need not have worried. Pilot Officer Cave was awarded the Distinguished Flying Cross for his courage in his attack on U 563, on 1 December 1941 just weeks after he left Limavady. On the 1 March 1942 now as a Flying Officer DFC he was again in action when he sank a trawler working with U-boats. Bill Cave DFC later reached the rank of Squadron Leader with 59 Squadron. Squadron Leader Cave was listed missing in 7 May 1943. His DFC was recently bought at a flea market in England.

Tony Spooner, who has written the foreword to this book, also stayed with the Grants, when with 221 Squadron. He remembers the late Mr. Grant well and Ian Grant remembers Tony and his wife. Mrs Spooner used to frequently play the flute, which caused no problems, but another lady did cause some eyebrows to be lifted as she practised her dancing including 'tap' on the bedroom floorboards between the edge of the carpet and the wall. Not only the guests got practice as Mr. Grant senior sharpened his powers of political persuasion with an eminent barrister who no doubt was keeping in shape for his return to civy life.

Wings Over The Foyle

Many others stayed at the farm house including an officer called Mills who played for Glentoran. Ian remembers his sports-car, particularly when Mills was going to sell it and after the deal was agreed gave the engine a 'rev up' only to have the con rod break and come through the side of the block.

Next door in Derrybeg house the Douglas' also kept RAF people. Mary Douglas recalls John Kirkpatrick and Alex Gibson from 502 Squadron. There was also an Admin. Officer named Berthon, from London, who's father taught French to the Royal Princes. Her own French text book had been edited by the same man. She also remembers a Rodrick Manhire and an Aeron Hughes who left about September 1944 and a family named Champion and the Carsons from 172 Squadron. There was also a Canadian called Mennie who was killed later in the war when he was with Bomber Command

But war is a time of tragedy as well as great excitement, not all of which is to do with the service people. One such tragedy was the death of a local boy Noel Millar, on 22 January 1943. John Wilson can remember, even though he was only a child, an aircraft overshooting the main runway and ending up at Alex Cochrane's old farmhouse at the end of the runway[3]. He ran to his grannies house and from the back of the next door neighbours, (an airforce family called Hans), he could see the tail of the Wellington sticking out of at a small sand-pit Barney Mullan was using for building sand. They rushed across and John remembers the pallor of the nose gunner as he climbed out with only a small cut above his eye. Very quickly the place was swarming with people and the air-crew were whisked away.

---

[3] The aircraft was most certainly HF860 crashed 16/1/43 at 13.25hrs. Pilot F/Sgt Carson

Wings Over The Foyle

The children, at school could not contain their excitement to get home and visit the aeroplane. On the Friday evening they left Gortnamoney as it was getting dark, after playing around the Wellington. Noel was getting perspex, about the only thing broken on the aircraft, to make rings some of which he had made and given to classmates. They said good-bye to Eileen Gordon who went home the other way (to what is now Barbers old house) and headed home. The boys were in the habit of skirting around the road security barrier between the cottages and the aerodrome and walking past the temporary guard accommodations there. Without saying anything Noel started hitting one of the huts. The others, thinking he was fooling around, walked on and John Wilson went home to the last house in the row. James McLaughlin coming home from work, was walking with the boys and saw nothing amiss. Markie, Noel's younger brother then turned round to get his big brother and returning to the spot they had last seen him, found him lying with his arms spread out. He was lifted, still with his scraps of perspex tucked under his coat and taken into a house(Stewarts), but despite their efforts was dead when the doctor arrived.

Speculation abounded as to the cause of death. Doctor Reid was unable to say immediately why he had died, it was thought he may have eaten something at the crash scene, however the other children had not seen him put anything in his mouth, or maybe the fire extinguish chemicals they had played with, were poisonous, the sample from John Wilsons coat ruled that out. The post-mortem showed Noel had indeed been poisoned, the substance metaldehyde, in soft pasty like form used for heating drinks while airborne, had caused asphyxiation; how he had ingested it was never fully explained.

Wings Over The Foyle

Although an exciting place for children, access for locals was controlled, however the controls were relaxed later. There was a guard hut and road barrier at Killane Bray on the outskirts of the town. The road people were used to from Magilligan through Aghanloo to Limavady was closed and they had to travel through Myroe. The council cottages at Dowland built in 1938 were practically inside the airfield area and the residents needed a pass to go in or out, Annie McCallion's pass for 1940/41 as reproduced here is an typical example. Although Lorna Picket (nee Atcheson) as a girl remembers driving out with her father and getting close enough to touch the aircraft.

> **AUTHORITY TO ENTER PROTECTED AREA.**
>
> NAME *Annie*
> ADDRESS *Dowland, Limavady*   *Annie McCallion*
> has permission to enter or be within or pass over the Protected Area of MAGILLIGAN, Co. LONDONDERRY,
> from *14th July 1940* to *14th January 1941* or until revoked.
>
> Signed *P. Hurst Lieut*

Limavady airfield closed after the war, its job done its last social fling on V.E. day. The end of season dance in the officers mess just happened to coincide with the historic day. The dance was attended by all including the Station Commander Group Captain Turner who had as a guest his son, a young Naval Officer. Mary Douglas at her first long dress formal danced the night away. When the dance ended they simply transferred to Limavady main street and partied to dawn, and still got up for work.

Wings Over The Foyle

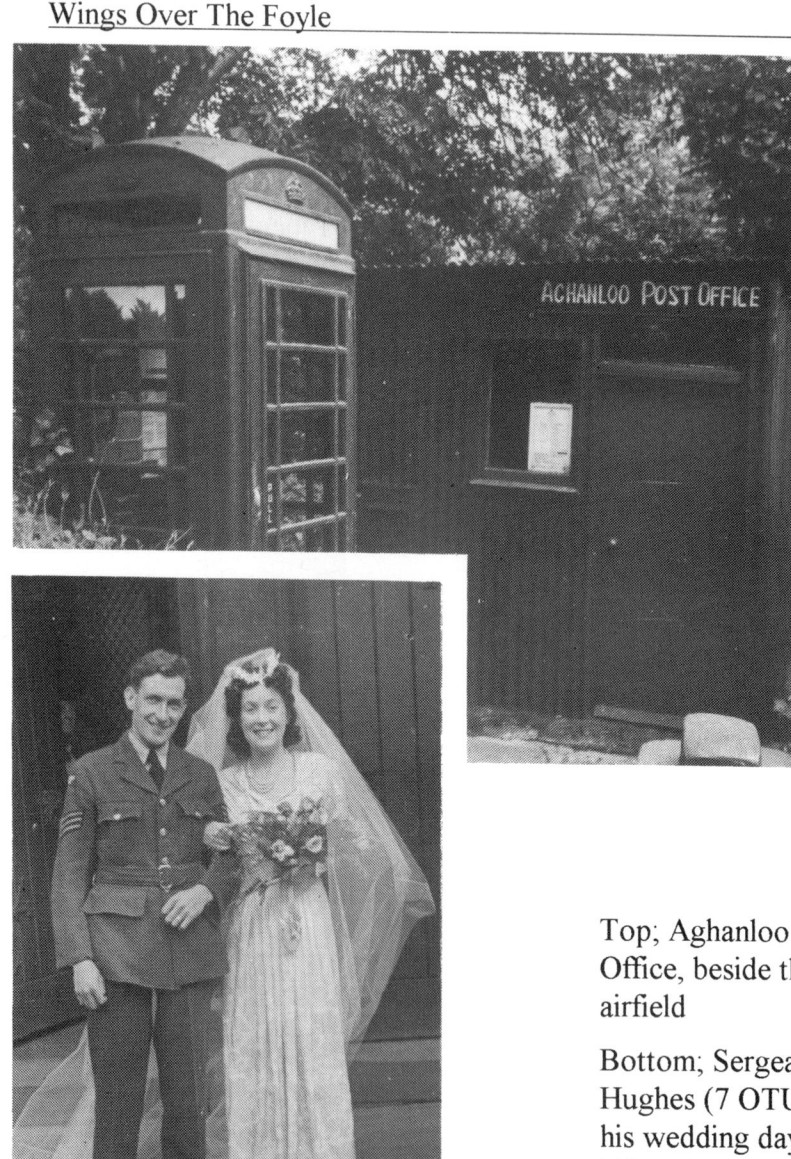

Top; Aghanloo Post Office, beside the airfield

Bottom; Sergeant Hughes (7 OTU) on his wedding day. He billeted with the Douglas' in Derrybeg House.

The Dogs of War.

Rover is seen here with Mrs. White who stayed with her husband at Derrybeg House

Rover appeared at Derrybeg House just after 502 Squadron were posted to Chivenor. It was obvious he had been attached to 502 or some other mess, because when a glass of beer was left on the ground by one of the airmen he immediately knew what to do. He drank it!. Maybe he should have transferred with 502, or maybe he knew when he was well off. He lived the rest of his natural life at Derrybeg, definitely not a casualty of war.

Tony Spooner also had a mascot a tiny pedigree Dandy Dinmont bitch named Jill. The local collie (being over sexed, and the tiny Dandy Dinmont being over here, as the saying goes), fathered a litter of pups. Ian Grant recalls with some amusement the shape of the unusual issue. When Tony was transferred to Malta, his wife took the Dandy Dinmont to England; he took both three week old pups with him in the aircraft. Their names were Harpic and Bonco (after the toilet disinfectant and toilet roll). The dogs were in the thick of it in Malta and got bomb shy and would

Wings Over The Foyle

make a dash for the bomb shelter at the first sign of bombs, of which there were plenty. They spent more and more time in the shelter and Tony lost contact with them.

The Crashes

Limavady airfield's location, in a strategic position for the Western Approaches was well suited for this purpose, but for the air-crew who had to fly out of in war-time conditions, the surrounding terrain proved hazardous.

Within the circuit lay Binevenagh Mountain, perched over the airfield, visible wherever you are; to the west Lough Foyle, County Donegal and the hills of Inishowen, and to the east the hills around the Roe Valley. This surrounding terrain claimed its toll of air-crew lives throughout the war.

In all the letters received from air-crew when putting this book together, reference was made to 'Ben Twitch'.. the wartime nickname for Binevenagh

No.221 Squadron's crash rate was very low, 502 Squadron was not so fortunate, twentyfour Whitleys went down overall, in operations, a listing of which can be found in this chapter. The locals remember the flying coffins- the slow aeroplane with the droning engines.

The Training Unit.

In April 1942 No. 7 OTU ((Coastal) Operational Training Unit) began training air-crew of that Command at Limavady with Wellingtons and Ansons. This OTU would remain at Limavady until January 1944 when it would move to Haversfordwest in Wales.

Tony Spooner, who had first came to Limavady with 221 Squadron returned in 1942 as an instructor with 7 OTU. He had spent six eventful months in Malta locating and shadowing

Wings Over The Foyle

German convoys, at night and had been awarded the DFC. Now back at Limavady with other 'veterans' they were teaching their skills to new crews. Other experienced flyers returned in this role and old 221 Squadron Limavady friends Squadron Leader Spooner, Squadron Leader Eric Starling and Squadron Leader 'Blisso' Ronnie Bliss (the group joker) worked together again. They laughed together and remember fondly Blisso's tongue in cheek lectures to the trainees on the evil of drink before flying. Before dismissing them he started stamping his feet on invisible objects, followed by comments of "Dammed black-beetles"

No. 7 (C)OTU were involved in N.A.V.E.Xs., Navigational Cross Country Exercises; advanced pupils were sent out to photograph Rockall, a bare rock hundreds of miles out in the Atlantic. Pupils were also trained to drop torpedoes as the Wellingtons had been modified to carry two.

During their time at Limavady, the OTU lost around twenty three aircraft in crashes. It is a high figure but when the number of sorties, for the twenty one months they were flying and the terrain is considered it was acceptable for wartime. Loss of aircrew in accidents is sad but morale was always high.

The sites of the majority of the Whitley and Wellington crashes listed in this chapter have been located and photographed over the years. It would be impossible, because of space to include photographs of them all in this book.

The Whitley Stories.

Of all the aircraft based in Limavady it is the Whitleys which bring wry smiles to the locals who remember, the comment 'flying coffins', usually accompanies the smile with a shake of the head. These aircraft had a reputation as an unsafe aircraft even

Wings Over The Foyle

among the non-airforce people. Many crashes and forced landings are remembered. John Barber remembers two such incidences, on one the Whitley came so close to his brothers house in Ballyhanna that it demolished a pile of timber John had to repair his roof.

The Armstrong Whitworth Whitley was first in service with No.10 Squadron in 1937. It was officially withdrawn as a bomber in mid 1942. The Mk V had a maximum speed of 230 mph. and a range of 1500 miles; it was powered by two Rolls Royce Merlin 1145 hp Merlin Mk X engines. For its defence it carried two .303 machine guns in the nose and four in the tail turret. From 1941 long range versions, the Mk. VII, fitted with ASV. radar served with Coastal Command as anti-submarine bombers.

In another incident people going to their work were surprised to see a Whitley in Alex Conner's field at Artikelly, just opposite the airfield gates. The pilot had somehow managed to get the aircraft down in a very confined space without damage to either plane or hedges. Ian Grant remembers very well the aircraft coming past very low on only one engine. He was out on his bicycle collecting for the Red Cross and saw it disappear over the trees near their house.

Further down the Derrybeg Road Mary Douglas was walking into the town, she was home from school in Coleraine where she was a weekday boarder. She saw the Whitley making its impossible landing on a slope difficult to walk up never mind land a plane on. She, fearing the worst, dashed towards the craft but was unable to cross the Curley Burn because of the height of the water. Mary dashed down stream to the bridge at Artikelly and up the river bank on Conner's side of the stream, only to get stuck in the marsh-land by the water edge. By this time she could

Wings Over The Foyle

see the crew making their way out of the aircraft, obviously fit and well.

The Whitley sat in the field for several weeks and it is remembered as looking like a large white seagull sitting on the hill. In order to salvage the aeroplane the recovery crew had only to trim a section hedge to below wing height and tow the aircraft out.(See photo page 114)

Hugh Mullan in Tullyarmon who lives just opposite the base hospital can point to the spot another Whitley ended up, it had been trying to takeoff and just not got off the ground. Some of McCloys men in a turnip field watched in amazement as the aeroplane ploughed through field and hedge coming to a stop where the Hospital was built. The crew clambered out no doubt thanking their lucky stars. Hugh can still picture the salvage crane trying to lift the Whitley after the salvage squad had removed the wings. The weight was too great and rather than lifting the aeroplane the crane nearly tipped over.

One crash is remembered by many people mainly because it occurred near the town and the load of bombs exploded. This aircraft had just taken off from Aghanloo with a full load and hit near Brolly's farm on the seacoast road. Mr. Brolly was quickly on the scene after the crash and was examining the wreckage when he was told it was loaded with bombs. He had barely taken shelter behind the lint stack when the plane exploded. Windows, not only at Brolly's but as far away as Killane Road, were broken. The Wilsons in Artikelly saw the flash and the two young boys John and Jim ran next door, to where the soldiers were billeted, thinking they were safer there.

The aircraft was Z6502 and the pilot, Sergeant Bagley, had avoided housing to make his landing. The aircraft hit the bottom of the hill which slowed it, then the tail snagged a lint stack which stopped it. All the crew were safe. The Captain of this aircraft was Flying Officer Collie, and he was involved in another crash not much more than a month later.

On the 24 November 1941, Flying Officer Collie and crew were returning to Limavady from an anti-submarine patrol when they had some difficulty getting an accurate 'fix' and over estimated their distance back to Limavady. They ran out of fuel just after they crossed the coast and had to crash land. They put the Whitley down at Moors farm in Risk, Priestland near Portrush. The pilot, according to Mrs. Moor's brother, spotted the farmhouse late in his approach, and just managed to lift the nose up for the aircraft to clear the house. Mrs. Moor was milking a cow at the time and the Whitley passed through the gap between the farmhouse and the outhouses, carrying away the house radio aerial, hitting the trees, breaking the branches 'as thick as a mans wrist' and ending up in a potato field with a wing on a potato pit.

The crew were looked after by the Moor's until they returned to base. An army guard was posted and stayed for some days. Mrs. Moors new Esse cooking range did a roaring trade in scones for some days, until the wreckage and guards left.

Pilot Officer Dickson

Pilot Officer Dickson of 502 Squadron had a rather traumatic time at, and on his way to, Limavady. Coming from Wick, on 13 February 1941, where he had been on detachment, the Whitley he was flying T4276 developed propeller trouble (it lost a blade) and the engine had to be stopped. When he was in Scotland the squadron had moved from Aldergrove to Limavady and he was going to Limavady for the first time. He had on board ground crew and luggage. As the aircraft was losing height and they were approaching the sea cliffs of the Butt of Lewis, everything movable was being dumped, personal luggage and everything else movable. Enough height was retained to get over the cliffs. They made it, but only just, and ditched in a lake on the other side.

Two months later on 27 April he took off from Limavady at 03.15hrs on an anti submarine patrol. He was Captain of Whitley Z6501 which was flown by Pilot Officer Carmichael. They no sooner had taken off when they developed engine problems and made the decision to return to base. However the airfield had switched off the lights and they couldn't easily estimate its or their position. Pilot Officer Dickson realised they were losing height in their endeavours to find the airfields. He called to Pilot Officer Carmichael to 'watch your height' but they were too late. Pilot Officer Carmichael managed to pull the aircraft up at the last minute but they hit Loughermore Mountain. Pilot Officer Dickson was knocked unconscious. The aircraft with a full load of petrol went on fire. Carmichael managed to get out and got round the other side and dragged Dickson free. All of the rest of the crew got out. They made some distance between themselves and the wreck as bullets were going off and bombs exploding. Dickson was quite badly burned and loosing blood from head wounds; Sergeant O'Connell was very badly burned.

Completely lost and suffering from shock 'possessing superhuman strength and intelligence' in reality being in a pretty poor state, the crew tried to make a plan. They assumed they had flown across the Lough and crashed on the Donegal Mountains, and they planned accordingly. Pilot Officer Dickson recalls, that as the Captain, he had quite a lot of money, issued for just such emergencies (to hire boats, etc.). He distributed it all, £400, among the crew and they set of to make their way home from, as they thought, Donegal. They split into two groups he leading one and Carmichael the other. Sergeant O'Connell was with Pilot officer Dickson and in a bad way. He had difficulty negotiating hedges and walls because of his burnt hands and he eventually passed out. Pilot Officer Dickson, fast loosing strength because of blood loss and the effect of the crash wearing off, eventually could not continue. Sergeant Redhead went on and soon came across a farm where help could be got. A party from the farm went back and carried the two injured in, using a gate as a stretcher. Pilot Officer Dickson can remember the farmer's wife taking one look at his blood stained and burned figure and fainting. Unusually for that time the house had a phone. The police at Eglinton were informed and they in turn informed the airfield. A lorry was sent for the crew and they were transported back to base at Limavady. Pilot Officer Dickson was determined to report back to the station commander Group Captain Pearce. Pilot Officer Tony Spooner from 221 just happened to be in the Nissan hut which served as an operations room when Dickson came in. He recalls the deathly white colour of the still shocked airman. The injured were taken to the town hospital, where Pilot Officer Dickson spent some time recovering.

He was posted out of Limavady but was later to return to Ballykelly with 86 Squadron on Liberators. He achieved some notoriety when he was in charge of a detachment detailed to meet the Irish Army escort of bodies of an RAF crew. Their Liberator, from 86 Squadron Aldergrove BZ802 'V', had crashed in Cork in August 1943. The Irish Army were escorting the bodies with full military honours and were scheduled to hand the bodies over at Beleek. Because of delays the hand over didn't take place until about three o'clock in the morning. The Irish detachments were a smart looking group and the officer in charge asked if Flight Lieutenant Dickson would inspect the Guard Of Honour. The

RAF detachment having being taken from other duties were not nearly as smart, but nevertheless the invitation to inspect then was given and accepted. It was then decided as the ranking Military Officer in Beleek that Flight Lieutenant Dickson had the authority to suspend the licensing laws and open the pubs, which he dully so declared. One pub was selected and after a promise was extracted from the men on both sides not to fight with one another, they all had a drink. Mindful of their duty when they were finished they solemnly reinstated the licensing laws before they left.

The Whitley

The Whitley was first in service in 1937. From 1941 long range versions, fitted with ASV. radar served with Coastal Command in an anti-submarine role. It was considered as an improvement on the aircraft Coastal Command had up to then. At the end of 1939 only one non flying boat squadron in the command had a modern type of aircraft, i.e. Hudsons. The Whitley, although earning a poor reputation for engine reliability, were better than the Ansons 502 Squadron used prior to this.

Not every Whitley and not every pilot had difficulty with the engines, some were lucky enough to have a relatively trouble free tour. However the conditions they were maintained in were such that even if the maintenance was a possible cause of a problem, to quote John Dickson a Pilot Officer with 502 [the pilots] "Could not fault the ground crew when one saw the conditions they have to work under".

Pilot Officer Dickson's difficulty resulting from a broken propeller, on his first flight to Limavady, was a common problem with Whitleys. Flight Lieutenant Hunter McGiffin as he was in early 1941, believes that in one day three Whitleys crashed because of it. During flight the tip of a propeller, the last six inches or so, would break off. This caused the engine to vibrate so much that it had to be shut down. The Whitley was under powered and had difficulty keeping aloft on one engine, particularly an ASV Whitley because of the extra drag.

The three crashes, Hunter McGiffin thinks occurred because of the propeller problem, were Z6553 (Corry's crash) and T4142 which ditched in the sea. The third was about the day of these two crashes. A Whitley got into difficulty at Limavady when it also had to shut down an engine. As it did not have enough height to circle the airfield, they had to land with the wind; this caused them to overshoot the runway and crash.

The fault was rectified by fitting new Rotol propellers.

Hunter McGiffin became an instructor with a Pilots Advanced Flying School (P)AFS, he went on to be a Wing Commander later in the war as an Officer Command of an small airfield in the Cotswolds. He then dropped a rank to come back to Northern Ireland, to Bishop's Court, as a Squadron Leader. After the war he was 502's Squadron Commander at Aldergrove.

The Tile Yard Hole

People can recall a crashed Wellington ending up with its nose in the water at the Tile Yard Hole at Aghanloo not more than fifty yards from the end of Limavady's runway. It was attempting to land. Hugh Mullan believes two crew died and he can remember unusually strict security around the wreck.

Another crash in the same area is recalled by Sydney Curry. He was cycling up the Murder Hole Road and saw a Swordfish which when flying low had hit a wire and crashed. Sydney also, as a young boy, was chased from a site of the crashed Wellington in the Drenagh estate on 5 May 1943 where they were looking for souvenirs. That aircraft had burned out; the crew of six unfortunately did not survive.

The Aeroplane Hole.

Another air crash which has left its stamp on the area and even changed the name of the countryside happened one spring evening in 1943. It was April, the start of the fishing season. Jim Wilson and Jack Irwin were fishing for white (sea) trout in the River Roe just below the end of the runway where the Hoechst social club now stands. They had just refitted their boots after wading across to the airfield side of the river when they heard an aircraft, a Wellington, coming down the runway with its engine running very roughly. They had no sooner made comment on this when the Wellington came in over their heads, it snagged the coiled barbed wire which marked the boundary of the airfield, and veering to the right plunged into the Roe. It hit a tall tree on the opposite bank and cut it so cleanly the tree landed on the airfield side. There were only two aboard, along with their seats, both were thrown clear(?). The burning fuel poured into the river and the Roe was set alight as the flow swept the flames round the bend. Fishermen, even the young who don't know why, still call the bend 'the Aeroplane Hole'. It is believed this was Wellington DV727 which crashed 3 April 1943.

Wings Over The Foyle

First Decoration for 502.

On 17 December 1941 Whitley P5054 was returning from patrol when it got into trouble. Nearly home it had to ditch in the sea off Castlerock. Sergeant Woods was the second pilot of the aeroplane and when it ditched he swam ashore and ran barefoot along the railway line until he came to an Army unit who were able to organise the rescue of his crew. Sergeant Woods was awarded the British Empire Metal for his gallantry and later rose to the rank of Squadron Leader.

First Training Fatalities.

Some times its the air-crew who are remembered rather than the crash. An Australian Sergeant Vernon Pither is one who is remembered very fondly. Not because the crash produced the first fatalities from the training squadron but because of Sergeant Pither.

Vernon was in the habit of visiting the Methodist Manse in Irish Green Street, where Mrs. Atcheson ran a tea and social evening on Sundays, and Lorna her daughter remembers Vernon. The evening was run on 'trust', that is the supplies of tea sugar, etc. were donated by the citizens of the town. They would go into Tweedy Atcheson shop and give a ounce of tea or sugar which mounted up until there was enough to keep the evening always supplied.

Vernon was, as usual at the social evening on Sunday but was complaining of not feeling well. The next day it appears he was ordered to accompany a New Zealand officer Pilot Officer Twentyman on a flight. He objected, maybe because he was unwell or maybe because there wasn't a full crew, (only he and the pilot were on the aircraft). Whatever the cause of the

105

objection it was of no avail, he had to obey orders and he was ordered to fly.

The Wellington crashed near Portrush on 20 July 1942, both occupants were killed.

Vernon's mates made a model from the perspex of the aircraft he had died in and gave it to the Atchesons to forward to his mother, in Australia, as a keepsake.

Later Vernon's brother came to Limavady to visit the war time friends his brother had made. He had shared his brothers interest in aerospace and had risen to senior position in Woomera Rocket Range. He was pleased to talk with those who had known and befriended Vernon while he was away from home.

All At Sea.

Flying Officer Brock in Whitley Z6635 call sign 'Q' from 502 Squadron took off from Limavady early on 17 July 1941 to escort convoy OB346 outward bound from Liverpool to Halifax, Nova Scotia. The convoy was about two hundred and fifty miles west of Ireland, when the Whitley, about five miles ahead of the convoy, spotted an aircraft. They assumed it to be a Hudson, from Aldergrove, also on escort duty.

Flying Officer Brock closed on the other aircraft in a shallow dive in order to make a positive identification. When they closed and made the signal of the day, it was not answered. By this time they were close enough to recognised the other aircraft as a Condor; the long range 'scourge of the Atlantic'. The FW 200 Condor, at the time was sinking as much shipping as were the submarines and they also acted as 'the eyes' of the U-boats directing the killer packs to their targets.

Wings Over The Foyle

The Whitley attacked the intruder starting to fire her forward guns from a range of about 250 yards. The first burst missed and the Condor returned fire and attempted to outrun the Whitley. Pilot Officer McLeod the second pilot who was operating the front guns continued firing and registered hits in the Condors fuselage. By this time the Condor was able to bring two gun positions to bear on the Whitley and succeeded in causing damage and wounding a 'passenger' Wing Commander Ross Shore the Officer Commanding the squadron. He was on board, possibly on a last flight with his squadron as he was due to transfer to 612 Squadron in Wick, or possibly actually in the process of transferring.

The Condor had the legs on a Whitley and the range extended until the Condor entered cloud. At this stage the Whitley could not continue the engagement because they had an overheating engine and they hadn't the speed. They were also fighting fires in the pyrotechnics and then the engine went on fire.

They turned back to the convoy and ditched the Whitley close to an escort vessel. The first world destroyer H.M.S. Wescott picked them up and tended to the injuries of the Wing Commander, Sergeant Hanson and Pilot Officer McLeod. Sergeant Larmour and Flying Officer Brock were uninjured. But the Condors were not finished with them.

Early the next day the Condors were back, this time not only to shadow the convoy but to attack. With the convoy was a CAM ship H.M.S. Maplin, the converted Fyffe banana boat Erin, which had been fitted with a rocket catapult to launch a Sea Hurricane. On the report of the presence of a Condor, Lieutenant Everettwas launched in Hurricane W9227 to intercept. The Condor attacked the 7,046 ton ship Pilar de Larrinaga machine gunning the decks and dropping a bomb on the saloon killing the Captain and three other members of the crew. The Pilar returned fire with its limited armaments scoring a hit. Meanwhile Everett in his Hurricane made a determine head on attack. But much to his frustration, just as he was about to press home his attack, the port wing of the Condor broke off as a result of hits by the defensive fire from the Pilar. Everett was left to fly to Northern Ireland to find a landing place as the Maplin or any CAM ship was not capable of landing aircraft.

The Wescott with the 502 Squadron crew aboard put alongside the Pilar to help fight the fire as the Pilar's pumps were out of order.

Later that night another Whitley from 502 Squadron Limavady Z6634 was carrying out an escort duty on the convoy. They also sighted a Condor which, on spotting them made off, with the Whitley in pursuit. The Whitley was no match for the speed of the German plane and it escaped before they could engage. On its return Z6634 piloted by Pilot Officer Lindsay, was diverted to Aldergrove. It overshot the runway, crashed and was written off; the crew were uninjured.

The Westcot escorted the Pilar under its own power, back to Belfast where the 502 air-crew from Z6635 could go ashore.

Whitley Z6553.   No.502 Squadron.

On 30 April 1941, Whitley Z6533 from 502 Squadron developed engine trouble on return from anti- submarine patrol. The aircraft was flown by Ulsterman, Squadron Leader Brian George Corry; his family run the Belfast timber company. Brian's brother Terance also with 502 Squadron was to become the Group

Wings Over The Foyle

Captain commanding a wing of Beaufighters in Iceland. The crew of Z6553 had to bale out and the aircraft crashed at Ashill in County Leitrim. All the crew were safe but not the top secret ASV. II; 502 were the first Squadron to have the new radar.

Concerned about the possibility of the radar getting into enemy hands, Squadron Leader Corry borrowed civilian clothes (an overcoat), from a lady who used to work for the family. In this dress he crossed the border as a civilian. The Gardia recognising him as an airman, but in acknowledgement of his civilian garb allowed him to approach the crashed aircraft. He was then able to smash the equipment and deny any possibility of secrets being revealed.

Crew; Squadron Leader Brian Corry (pilot), Pilot Officer Geoffrey Markham-Jones (co-pilot), Sergeant Bailey; Sergeant Robert Eaton, Sergeant Reginald Graham.

Wings Over The Foyle

Top; John Wilson points out to Dan Reilly where a 7 OTU Wellington (DV727) crashed in April 1943 after overshooting.

Bottom; The price paid; Sergeant Vernon Pither and Pilot Officer Twentyman are buried at Christchurch, Drumachose.

Wings Over The Foyle

Top;   The Tileyard Hole, at the end of a runway, with Binevanagh in the background; a 7 OTU Wellington ended up in here.

Bottom; 1990. John Woods (left) and John Quinn on the crash spot at Ashill. No visible sign remain to show a war time bomber crash.

Wings Over The Foyle

An early 'Prang'. Skeen Co. Sligo.

Top; John Quinn at the spot in Skeen, County Sligo where Hudson, of 224 Squadron crashed landed in 24 January 1941. The four crew were interned. The Hudson later became the Irish Presidents Transport.

Bottom; According to one local, when asked in 1990, one of the crew was in the Jersey Bar when the local security forces arrived. The bar has survived in name only.

Wings Over The Foyle

A No.502 Squadron Whitley taken at Limavady in 1940, note ASV aerials. Possibly Connor's field? (Photo H McGiffin)

No. 502 Squadron Whitley Crashes.

Date	Serial no.	
7 December 1940.	T4277 J	Took off at 18.35 hrs on an anti submarine patrol, crashed approximately fifteen minutes later; crew, Flight Lieutenant Rees. Pilot Officer Wortherton. Sergeant Millar. (WirelessOperator/ Air Gunner);.Sergeant Adams (Navigator); Sergeant Brown (Wireless Operator /Air Gunner) Sergeant Brown seriously injured. All others killed.
23 January 1941	T4168	Illes, four miles N/W of Buncrana, Co. Donegal. Returning from anti-submarine patrol. Pilot Officer Ward, Flight Sergeant Jefferson, Sergeant Johnston, Sergeant Hogg, Sergeant Greenwood -(Air Gunner) three killed (see page 121).
23 January 1941	P5041	Near Campbeltown, Scotland. Flight Lieutenant Billing, Flying Officer Holmes, Sergeant Hooker, Sergeant Pilling, Sergeant, Bradley ,all killed.
7 February 1941	T4223	Crashed position 55.30N 10.55W; Ditched in the sea all crew picked up. Crew, Flight Lieutenant Henderson, Injured; Flying Officer Holdsworth, Injured, Sergeant Graham, Injured; Sergeant Banner Injured; Sergeant Eaton uninjured.

Wings Over The Foyle

Date	Aircraft	Details
10 February 1941	T4320	Crashed at 0820 hrs Position Half-a-Mile south Ballintrae house, Port Ballintrae,(on the Bush River) crew: Squadron leader Stanley, Sergeant Wood, Sergeant Matthews, Sergeant Hollins, all uninjured.
13 February 1941	T4276	Crashed on returning from Wick, all crew uninjured. Flight Lieutenant Foster, Pilot Officer Dickson, Sergeant Buckley, L.A.C. Douglas, L.A.C. Frazer. time 12.30 hrs(see also Z6501).
18 February 1941	P5107	When taking off at Limavady, the aircraft hit an obstruction on the aerodrome and crashed with no injuries. Crew Wilkinson, Sergeant Spurgeon, Sergeant Martin, Sergeant Evans, Sergeant McGrath, Sergeant Bone.
5 March 1941	P5010	When taking off at Limavady, the aircraft hit an obstruction on the aerodrome and crashed at 08.25 hrs on the foreshore of Lough Foyle with no injuries (cat E crash) Crew Pilot Officer Paterson, Sergeant Morrison, Sergeant Norman, Sergeant Smith, Sergeant Sowyer.
11 March 1941	T4222	Flying Officer Preston because of engine trouble ditched at sea all crew picked up.
12 March 1941	P5045	Galway Bay returning from a anti-submarine patrol. Two crew baled out and survived, Pilot Officer Midgley and Sergeant Harkell, all others killed; Pilot

		Officer Dear, Pilot Officer Edwards, Sergeant Goodlett.
27 April 1941	Z6501	Aircraft was airborne at 03.15 from Limavady, flown by Pilot Officer Carmichael, but a short time later crashed into a hillside south of the Derry road, at Glasakeeran on the west of Loughermore Mt. The aircraft caught fire and its bombs exploded, but all the crew had escaped. Sergeant O'Connell the observer was badly burned, Pilot Officer Dickson the aircraft captain was burned and had a lacerated scalp. The other crew members were slightly burned, but OK. At 07.00 hrs Pilot Officer Dickson reached the operations room at Limavady and reported to Group Captain Pearce. At 08.56 hrs all crew were taken to Roe Valley Hospital, Limavady after treatment at the station. Crew Pilot Officer Dickson, Pilot Officer Carmichael, Sergeant O'Connell (Navigator), Sergeant Dorney (w/t) Sergeant Redhead (w/t) Sergeant Wilson (Air Gunner).
??	P5096	Crashed while on detachment to Wick.
29 April 1941	T4142	Ditched of the island of Barra in the Hebrides, all crew O.K.
30 April 1941	Z6553	Crashed at Ashill County Leitrim 04.00 hrs Pilot returned to the aircraft to destroy ASV. (see page 108) Crew;

		Squadron Leader Corry, Pilot Officer Howard Jones, Sergeant Eaton,(nav) Sergeant Banner (w/t), Sergeant Graham (w/t).
17 July. 1941	Z6635 'Q'	On escort duty with outward bound convoy OB346. Ditched in the sea after conflict with a Condor F.W.200, The Condor was damaged. The crew were picked up uninjured by HMS Westcott. Crew Pilot Officer Brock, Flying Officer McLeod, Sergeant Lormour, Sergeant Hanson. Also on board Officer Commanding; Wing Commander Ross Shore.(see page 106).
19 July 1941	Z6634 'K'	Returning from an anti-submarine patrol escorting outward bound convoy OB346 and an encounter with a Condor (F.W. 200), unable to land at Limavady and was instructed to land at Aldergrove. When attempting to land the aircraft overshot the aerodrome and crashed. All uninjured. Crew; Flying Officer Lindsay, Sergeant Bell, Pilot Officer Mearns, Sergeant Millington, Sergeant Manning, Sergeant Brown.
23 August 1941	Z6500 'Q'	Crashed in the vicinity(one mile west) of the base when returning from escort duties. Weather not more than 5/10 cloud with base at 1000-2000 ft. Visibility good. Flying Officer Sproule, Sergeant Naylor

117

19 October 1941	Z6502 'U'	2nd pilot, Pilot Officer Matthews Navigator, Sergeant Jones Wireless Operator all killed Lieutenant Bevan RNVR. From HMS Watchman, on board for air experience also killed. Sergeant Monk (injured), Sergeant Bradshaw (injured). This aircraft took off on an anti-submarine patrol at dawn. The take which was made by the 2nd pilot Sergeant Bagley, was normal until the aircraft reached approx. 50 ft, when the starboard engine misfired, fired again momentarily and then ceased. It was found that the application of the petrol cocks was correct the boost cut-out control was pulled by the pilot to obtain extra power from the port engine, but by this time the airspeed had dropped to 80 knots and at this low speed he was unable to maintain height or keep the aircraft straight on one engine. By skilful piloting he avoided hitting any of the houses or trees, and just managed to pull the aircraft up a steep slope before it stalled completely, two miles South West of the airfield. C912539 He was unable to jettison the bombs because of the inhabited outskirts of Limavady. Aircraft destroyed by fire. Capt. Flying Officer Collie.

Wings Over The Foyle

24 October 1941	P5059	Ditched at sea all crew picked up.
24 November 1941	Z6967 'U'	Detailed to escort a convoy and was airborne at 08.41 hrs the convoy was not met and at 14.02 hrs. the aircraft was recalled to base. At 16.18 land was sighted in poor visibility. this was thought to be the southern extremities of the Hebrides, but was in fact the Flanner Islands, further north west course was reset several times and D.F. fix from Renfewn indicated that the position at 17.25 was an hour from base. Petrol shortage became apparent. Depth charges were jettisoned and SOS was sent out at 18.20 hrs, the engines failed at 18.48 hrs the aircraft was then at 1,800 ft approaching the hills between Castlerock and Limavady. The Capt. Flying Officer Collie landed in a field near Priestland, five miles south east of Portrush. No injuries.
27 November 1941	P5050 'T'	Collided with a light army truck at 13.30 hrs while being taxied along the perimeter track in heavy rain. A rib of the starboard mainplane and starboard flap and the leading edge of the tailplane were damaged. The Capt. Pilot Officer Brown was relying on the second pilot keeping a lookout, but his attention at the moment

119

9 December 1941	Z9190	was distracted by notifying a failure of inter-comm.[4] Undershot the east-west runway while making a practice landing. The port under-carriage fouled the hedge of the outer perimeter track and collapsed causing the aircraft to swing left and go off the runway. Pilot Officer Harris No fatalities.[5]
17 December 1941	P5054	Crashed in the sea off Castlerock, all crew picked up, due to the actions of Sergeant Woods (see page 105).

---

[4] P5050 Ditched of the french coast 4 Feb 1942 and the crew and Squadron Leader Davies the Capt were made POWs

This aircraft was also flown by Flying Officer Walker when he damaged U93 on 11 Feb 1941

[5] This was the same aircraft used by Flying Officer Holdsworth to sink U206 30 November 1941, just nine days earlier.(see main text)

Wings Over The Foyle

Whitley T4168

On January 25th, 1941 two aircraft from Limavady came down in Eire. The second was Whitley T4168 of 502 Squadron, this aircraft was returning from an anti-submarine patrol when it got into difficulty. At the controls was Pilot Officer Ward, an RAF regular from Vancouver. The aircraft encountered the west coast of Ireland south of Galway; they got their location when they recognised three islands to the south of the Arran Islands. The aircraft received call signals from Tory and Malin but could not find Innistrahul Lighthouse; it is essential to find this beacon to allow navigation to Limavady airfield. They crossed to the Scottish coast and re-crossed to Ireland looking for bearings. They had overshot the drome when they saw the fairy lights and were about to turn the aircraft when fuel ran out. The aircraft had been lost for three hours. Normally the aircraft would have done an eight hour patrol, carrying eight hundred gallons of fuel.

After they had recognised Derry city, Pilot Officer Ward ordered the crew to bale out, the aircraft was over Lough Foyle at this stage. Flight Sergeant Johnston was the first to go, his father-in-law, a Squadron Leader had already been killed in a crash. Among the first three out was the wireless operator Fight Sergeant Jefferson from Belfast. The last to go was Pilot Officer Ward, the pilot, leaving the aircraft to fly on over Inishowen.

The aircraft was the second Northern Ireland based aircraft to crash in Eire in twenty four hours, the first being the 224 Squadron Hudson at Skreen in Sligo. This Hudson forced landed and was repaired and converted. It became quite well known as President DeValera personal transport.

121

Wings Over The Foyle

The Whitley crashed into rising ground on Glenard Hill, in the Illes, four miles west of Buncrana. Three of the crew were drowned in Lough Foyle, only one of whom, Sergeant Johnston, was recovered. His body was washed in on the Donegal side of the lough near Moville. Pilot Officer Ward, and Belfast man Flight Sergeant Jefferson landed safely, Ward coming down near the plane and injuring his left leg. He made his way to a nearby house, that of an ex R.I.C. man. Local people gathered around the house, and three members of the Local Defence Force arrived from Buncrana, but the R.I.C. man would not hand Pilot Officer Ward over until the Gardai and Army arrived.

I have been told, Pilot Officer Ward only had one thing in mind, and that was to get across the border. One local man told me, had he got him, he would have brought him to the border. From this house he was taken by Gardai to Buncrana, and at 06.00 hours on the 25th he and Sergeant Jefferson were taken into Military Custody. While in Gardai custody, much to the dismay of Irish Army G2, the two crewmen had managed to phone the operations room at Limavady. Both men were subsequently interned in the Curragh.

This Whitley was one of the first to be fitted with the then secret ASV. II radar and latest bomb sight and according to Flight Sergeant Jefferson, Pilot Officer Ward was worried they may be discovered. But they were destroyed in the crash. Two of the aircraft's bombs exploded on impact and pieces of the aircraft was scattered over a mile of countryside. The aircraft crashed into bog land at a steep angle and the two engines lay 6 to 10 feet deep, they were not recovered. A large quantity of .303 ammunition was lost in the bogs; some had fallen into civilian hands, Gardai reported successfully retrieving it. Two remaining bombs were blown up on site.

The surface remains of the aircraft was carted to Buncrana along with salvaged aluminium from the 271 Squadron Blenheim from Aldergrove, which crashed at Slidrum Glen on 21st December 1940. There was, in all, nearly six tons of wreckage.

During ground research on Donegal aircraft wrecks, I discovered plans were in progress, with official permission, to excavate the aircraft's two engines. A local man now living in Australia was behind the venture. He wanted them out to work and restore, purely because of an interest in engines. I asked to be contacted when the dig was due to take place, and voiced a case to his friend who was handling matters from Buncrana, for one of the engines to come North, this was in March 1990.

The Dig On Whitley T4168
502 SQUADRON - LIMAVADY
SEPTEMBER 1990

With only a telephone call the night prior to the dig taking place, as notice, I quickly put together some gear, and set off at 11pm to drive up to Buncrana, via the A6. Robert, who was driving, and I reached our destination at 3am, after a detour back to Belfast for my camera; I had forgotten it in the rush. The rest of the night was spent in the White Strand Hotel, on the outskirts of Buncrana. Robert had to drive back to Belfast for work in the morning.

I ordered breakfast for 7.30am and at 8.05am Patsy Doherty with Packy McGonigle, picked me up, as arranged. Patsy Doherty had been responsible for setting up the dig, laying the groundwork, writing for information and official permission etc.

Wings Over The Foyle

Patsy would attend the dig, but his job was done. The man behind the venture, paying the worker's and footing the finances, was former local man, now living in Australia, and a retired aeronautical engineer, Barney Bradley.

Barney like Patsy, as a young man, remembered an aircraft crashing in the Illes. He had always wanted to retrieve the engine and restore it. He knew nothing of the type of aircraft, or the story behind it, until I told him, nor would he believe there were two engines. In fact the truth of the matter is, Barney would not have recognised a Whitley if it landed beside him. His opinion was that the aircraft was a single engine fighter, a Hurrican or some such which would not have a Merlin X.

Out in the Illes a tracked digger, owned by Colm Grant, had been hired for the dig. (I had met Colm early in the year, during my research), and a local man, Sean McGonigle, Packy's son, and a few others were present. Digging a crash site was a completely new experience for them, but it must be said, that they did an excellent job.

Colm was an expert with his digger, and Sean worked very hard. All round, they were a very good team of men. Sean took us up to the site on a four-wheeled tractor and trailer, we proceeded about 250 yards into the forest where work commenced with a Sthil saw cutting a track out for the digger. The branches acted as an extra base for the digger over what was once, and still is boggy marshland. With Barney now on the scene, work was under way. The whole operation was filmed on video by a local man, John Friel, also hired by Barney. The dig began with tangled pieces of wreckage being scooped out, as we guided Colm where to direct the scoop. Barney and I got on well, at first, we consulted as various pieces began to come out. We had

Wings Over The Foyle

gone about three feet down when Barney began to voice doubt as to the presence of an engine. I assured him that the engine was there and we had not gone deep enough, we continued to dig. More tangled wreckage came out, then at 6 feet the first prominent piece, an undercarriage leg and burst wheel were recovered. The emergence of fuel lines gave hope to Barney of an engine. At over 8 feet, the depth that I had predicted, we had the engine.

A Whitley V bomber was powered by two Rolls Royce Merlin X engines, however no matter how often I told Barney that they were Merlin X engines, he was convinced that they were Merlin XII's. I do not think even at this stage, he believed he was digging on a Whitley. This was the only crashed aircraft that Barney knew of in Co Donegal. He had undertaken no research into the Whitley as an aircraft, it's history, or squadron or "crashes" in the county.

Sean McGonigle, working up to his eyes in muck, and Colm earned their money by the effort put into getting the engine out of what was now a water-filled crater. The engine out and Merlin X clearly stamped on the block plate, it was now into tea-time, a days work had been done. I put it to Barney about going for the second engine. It stood to reason that it was there, even Barney should see that!. It was decided to go for it the next day, Saturday.

Earlier on Friday, Hugo, who owns the Square Bar in Clonmany, turned up at the site, and spent the day taking photographs. What also developed during the dinner break, was the first sign of Barney's views and intentions to "sell the story" of the dig to the national media. John had not been hired with the video just for Barney to have a memento in his old age!. Signs began to appear of a commercial venture mixed with a genuine interest in aircraft engines. I got the impression that Barney thought he was engaged in 'a first' digging up of Rolls Royce engines. Had he done his 'homework' he would have discovered that aviation groups and museums have been engaged in such operations for years without any commercial gains. People do this through a 'genuine interest', without any financial rewards. Looking back, with hindsight, I should have encouraged him to stop there and then, with his engine recovered.

The following day Barney would get publicity, but not because of his engines. It was to be the kind of publicity that researchers find counter-productive, and like to avoid.

Friday evening, I went back to Clonmany with Barney and Hugo, and booked in to a B & B. Saturday morning had us back at the site and we began probing elsewhere in the hope of locating the second engine. A first detection with the probe proved, after Colm had re-positioned the digger, to be a prop boss and reduction gear wheel, something Barney was after. Following this, problems began, trying to locate the second engine. We decided on an area and the digger began. Sean and I probed the new crater for any signs of the engine. Barney, only at this stage and probably based on my record so far, began to believe in the 'second engine'.

During the operation I noticed the top of a yellow cylindrical object, in an upright position, peering out of the mud. I shouted on Colm to stop the digger. Sean and myself began to clean away the mud to try and identify, what might be a bomb. Others had come over to the crater like hole. In the back of my mind I was worried. I knew it could be a bomb, but was quick to dismiss the possibility, in order to reassure those present, although there was an overall calmness among everyone. We were careful, we knew we had to take it out in order to make a positive identification, before any action could be taken such as call in the Army for disposal.

Sean and I tied a rope and in a delicate operation Colm slowly lifted the object from the mud, revealing a 250lb bomb. Despite all the records in the Irish Military Archives having reassure me of their disposal of all bombs at the time, here was a very 'present' and live bomb made up of 250lb of T.N.T. There was a very calm and easy going approach to the whole situation, even to the point that the local gardai did not cordon off the area; that is until the Irish Army got involved. They took a more serious approach.

Such a find may have created a 'buzz' in the locality, but for a researcher, in wreckology, such finds are counter productive. This is when the media take an interest!. Perhaps for Barney it would have given him an added angle to his venture, but for me it was an unwanted distraction. Patsy Doherty had always been wary of the official reports relating to the bombs; he was right!. The dig would be postponed now whilst the Irish Army would do their bit and finish the job they started, after the crash, some 50 years ago.

The following day (Sunday), Robert and I returned to Belfast and my work was done!. Patsy Doherty described Robert and I as 'amateur professionals', a compliment!. Relations with Barney became strained, from him there was no thanks. After our return to Belfast, Barney and the team were allowed to continue the dig and excavate the second engine. It, along with all the wreckage was crated back to Clonmany. The promised engine was never given to us for eventual display in the North, either in Belfast or

Wings Over The Foyle

the North West where it properly belonged. Even the wreckage which Barney had no interest in was held.

I have had no contact since with Patsy or Barney. They were a good bunch of lads, and I enjoyed the few days with them and Patsy.

Crash listings and Roll of Honour.

A Listing of Wellington crashes.

(Aircraft all operating out of Limavady)

This attempt is complete as far as we can research when going to press, no doubt there are omissions.

SER N	CRASH LOCATION	DATE	UNIT	C	Pilot
W5653	URRIS HILLS/CROAGHCARRAGH	11/04/41	221 SQ	6	P/O Cattley
W5615	LOUGH FOYLE, 2MLS S.W. OF MAGILLIGAN POINT	12/05/41	221 SQ	6	F/O Robinson
W5659	ST KILDA AREA	22/06/41	221 SQ	6	P/O Johnson
?????	LOST NEAR SCILLY ISLES	11/07/41	221 SQ	6	F/O Sanderson
?????	FAILED TO RETURN	17/08/41	221 SQ	6	F/L Cakebread
DV228	SWUNG OFF RUNWAY ON TAKE OFF BURNT OUT	07/07/42	7 O.T.U.		
DV728	AIRFIELD DISPERSAL, SWUNG ON TAKEOFF.	12/07/42	7 O.T.U.		
DV772	GIANTS CAUSEWAY	20/07/42	7 O.T.U.	2	P/O Twentyman
T2919	COAL HILL,3 MLS EAST OF THE AIRFIELD	12/08/42	7 O.T.U.	3	
R1533	RAN OFF RUNWAY ON NIGHT LANDING	31/08/42	7 O.T.U.		
R1021	FORCED LANDED CHARLEVILLE Co.CORK	26/09/42	7 O.T.U.		
HX448	LOST ON EXERCISE TO PHOTO ROCKALL ST. KILDA	28/09/42	7 O.T.U.	6	Sgt Hutton
W5713	BINEVENAGH	02/01/43	7 O.T.U.		
HX439	SISTRAKEEL,2MLS S.W. BALLYKELLY	02/01/43	7 O.T.U.	4	

HX467	LOUGH FOYLE	02/01/43	7 O.T.U.	6	
HF860	OVERSHOT RUNWAY, CRASHED GORTNAMONEY	16/01/43	7 O.T.U.		F/Sgt Carson
HX420	CRASHED ON NIGHT LANDING	31/01/43	7 O.T.U.	5	
HX737	GORTNACHOICE CO. DONEGAL	27/02/43	7 O.T.U.	7	
LB112	CRASHED ON LANDING	07/03/43	7 O.T.U.		
DV727	STALLED ON OVERSHOOTING RUNWAY	03/04/43	7 O.T.U.	2	
LB241	DRENAGH ESTATE AFTER TAKEOFF	05/05/43	7 O.T.U.	6	Sgt Holden
HX477	LOUGH FOYLE	17/05/43	7 O.T.U.	6	Sgt Baker
HF902	CAUGHT FIRE, BURNED ON DISPERSAL	29/05/43	7 O.T.U.		
HX424	STRUCK MARKER BALL OF No 1 TARGET	04/07/43	7 O.T.U.		
HF838	DICKEYS GLEN, BOLEA	13/07/43	7 O.T.U.	5	
HZ178	CRASHED INTO HE416 ON LANDING	21/08/43	7 O.T.U.		
HE302	FORCED LANDED AT BELLARENA	07/09/43	7 O.T.U.		
LB243	DITCHED 1 MILE OFF PORTRUSH	16/09/43	7 O.T.U.		
W5647	SCAWL HILL, nr BALLYGAWLEY ANTRIM	17/09/43	7 O.T.U.		
R1504	DITCHED 2 MILES NORTH OF DOWNHILL	30/10/43	7 O.T.U.		
LB247	HIT HILL EAST OF LIMAVADY	05/11/43	7 O.T.U.	1	

Wings Over The Foyle

DV597	DITCHED OFF PORTBALLINTRAE	08/11/43	7 O.T.U.	
DV664	DIVED INTO THE SEA OFF PORTBALLINTRAE	28/11/43	7 O.T.U.	
HF142	STALLED ON TAKEOFF, CAUGHT FIRE ON IMPACT	14/02/44	407SQ	5 1st/Lt Blesser
HF450	GALWAY BAY, SALT HILL	05/10/44	172SQ	1

A list of Whitley crashes;

Aircraft operating from Limavady.
We have attempted to make this listing as accurate as possible but inevitable crashes will have been omitted.

SER No	CRASH LOCATION	DATE	UNIT	C	Pilot
T4277 J	15 MIN FROM TAKEOFF LIM.	07/12/40	502 Sqn.	4	F/L Rees
T4168	BUNCRANA	23/01/41	502 Sqn.	3	P/O Ward
P5041	CAMPBELTOWN	23/01/41	502 Sqn.	5	F/L Billing
T4223	AT SEA CREW INJURED	07/02/41	502 Sqn.	0	F/L Henderson
T4320	PORT BALLINTRAE	10/02/41	502 Sqn.	0	S/L Stanley
T4276	IN A LAKE ON BARRA	13/02/41	502 Sqn.	0	P/O Dickson
P5107	ON TAKEOFF LIM.	18/02/41	502 Sqn.	0	Wilkinson

132

Wings Over The Foyle

P5010	ON TAKEOFF LIM.	05/03/41	502 Sqn.	0	P/O Paterson
T4222	DITCHED AT SEA, ENGINE	11/03/41	502 Sqn.	0	P/O Preston
P5045	GALWAY BAY	12/03/41	502 Sqn.	3	P/O Dear
Z6501	SOUTH OF DERRY RD. LIM.	27/04/41	502 Sqn.	0	P/O Carmichael
T4142	DITCHED OF BARRA	29/04/41	502 Sqn	0	
Z6553	ASHILL	30/04/41	502 Sqn.	0	S/L Corry
?	BROKEN PROP OVERSHOT R/WAY	30/04/41	502 Sqn	0	
Z6635	AT SEA, CONFLICT WITH FW200	17/07/41	502 Sqn	0	P/O Brock
Z6634	OVERSHOT R/W ALDERGROVE	19/07/41	502 Sqn.	0	F/O Lindsay
Z6500 'Q'	1 ML. WEST OF AIRFIELD LIM.	23/08/41	502 Sqn.	4	F/O Sproule
Z6502 'U'	NR AIRFIELD FORCED LANDING	19/10/41	502 Sqn.	0	Sgt Bagley
P5059	DITCHED AT SEA. CREW OK	24/10/41	502 Sqn	0	
Z6967 'U'	PRIESTLAND PORTRUSH	24/11/41	502 Sqn.	0	F/O Collie
P5050 'T'	WHEN TAXIING LIM	27/11/41	502 Sqn.	0	P/O Brown
Z9190	WHEN LANDING LIM.	09/12/41	502 Sqn.	0	P/O Harris
P5054	IN THE SEA OFF CASTLEROCK	17/12/41	502 Sqn.	0	
P5096	WHILE ON DETACHMENT WICK	??	502 Sqn	?	

133

Wings Over The Foyle

Other Crashes

SER No	CRASH LOCATION	TYPE	DATE	UNIT	C	Pilot
AM539	SWUNG ON TAKEOFF	HUDSON	24/09/41	224		
V9112	CROCKANEEL, 1527 SQN.BEAM APP.TRAIN FLIGHT.	HUDSON	12/04/42	44(FC)	3	Matson
?	LIMAVADY AIRFIELD	BLENHEIM	23/04/42	143		
L9948	BALLYKELLY	BLENHEIM	25/04/42	143		
V5447	ALDERGROVE	BLENHEIM	01/05/42	143		
P4835	BURST TYRE ON TAKE OFF	BLENHEIM	22/05/42	143		
V5561	BURST TYRE ON TAKE OFF	BLENHEIM	29/05/42	143		
WI706	BURST TYRE ON TAKEOFF BUT CRASH LANDED	ANSON	13/07/42	7OTU		
HN871	?	MARTINETS	21/08/43	?		
HP166	CRINDLE 1 ML N.W. OF THE AIRFIELD	MARTINETS	22/08/43	?		P/O Fowler
NR896	LIMAVADY	SWORDFISH	14/07/44	811	1	S/Lt Cassels
?	TULLYARMON NAAFI AREA	SWORDFISH	?	FAA?		
?	FARLOW WOODS	SWORDFISH	?	FAA?		

134

Wings Over The Foyle

Roll of Honour.

(A list of those killed while operating out of Limavady).

Often those who could were buried in their home towns, this explains the majority of war graves in Limavady being those of Commonwealth Airmen. The fatalities from the operational Squadron were to a large extent lost at sea, in many instances the bodies were not recovered and as such have no known grave. There is a war memorial at Runnymede which has an inscription of each airman who has no known grave. The names of those lost out of Limavady who did not return are listed here. Some graves in Limavady church are from airmen who operated out of other airfields, these are included in this list simply to avoid confusion and to let those visiting these graves distinguish between graves of people from Limavady (Aghanloo) and the others. A '?' in the crash column means not operating out of Limavady Airfield or we are not sure.

This list does try to include everyone who died while operating from Limavady but inevitable some will have been left out. The 7 OTU unit which crashed while training on other bases are not included even though they were 'Limavady' units, and Fleet Air Arm units casualties, are mostly not included.

135

Surname	Initials	Rank	Date killed	Age	Airforce	Buried	Sqn	Crashed
ADAMS	W.A.	SGT NAV	07/12/40		RCAF	?	502	15 MIN FROM AERODROME
ADAMS	H.W.	SGT	28/09/42		RCAF	NOT RECOVERED	7OTU	SEA OFF ST.KILDA
ANDERSON	R.W.	SGT P	05/05/43	21	RAF	CHRISTCHURCH	7OTU	DRENAGH
ANDERSON	J.G.	F/O NAV	13/07/43	24	RNZAF	CHRISTCHURCH	7OTU	DICKEY GLEN
BADMAN	B.L.	SGT	11/04/41		RAF(VR)	PONTYPOOL	221	URRIS HILLS
BAILLARGEON	P.E.R.	SGT	19/06/44		RCAF	St.MARY'S	59	OUT OF BALLYKELLY
BAKER	H.J.	SGT	12/08/42		RAF(VR)	CHRISTCHURCH	7OTU	COAL HILL
BAKER		SGT	17/05/43			?	7OTU	LOUGH FOYLE
BATEMAN	J.W.H.	SGT	11/04/41	30	RAF(VR)	SUTTON BRIDGE	221	URRIS HILLS
BERGER	C.B.	SGT	31/01/43	24	RAAF	CHRISTCHURCH	7OTU	NIGHT LANDING
BEVAN		LT	23/08/41		RN	?	RN	MYROE
BILLING		F/LT P	23/01/41			GLENAVY	502	CAMPBELTOWN
BIRTILL	H.R.	SQN LDR	20/04/45	30	RAF(VR)	CHRISTCHURCH		?
BLESSER	D.B.	1st/LT	14/02/44		USAAF?	?	407	STALLED AFTER T/O
BOHAM	F.L.	FLT/SGT	12/05/41	19	RAF	NOT RECOVERED	221	LOUGH FOYLE
BRADLEY		SGT	23/01/41			?	502	CAMPBELTOWN
BRIDGE		P/O	17/05/43			?	7OTU	LOUGH FOYLE
BUTLAND	F.D.	F/O WOP/AG	13/07/43		RCAF	CHRISTCHURCH	7OTU	DICKEY GLEN
CAKEBREAD	C.	F/LT	17/08/41		RAF	NOT RECOVERED	221	DID NOT RETURN
CAMPBELL	A.N.	F/L	10/12/44	26	RAF(VR)	PRESBYTERIAN CHURCH	575	SHROPSHIRE
CASS	W.E.	FLT/SGT	22/06/41		RAF(VR)	NOT	221	DID NOT

136

Wings Over The Foyle

						RECOVERED		RETURN
CASSELS	R.B.	SUB LT	14/07/44	21	RNVR	FAUGHANVALE PRES.	811	LIMAVADY AIRFIELD
CAITLEY	A.P.	F/O	11/04/41	24	RAF	GOLDERS GREEN	221	URRIS HILLS
CLARK	J.	SGT WOP/AG	31/01/43	20	RAF(VR)	St.MARY'S	7OTU	NIGHT LANDING
CLARKE	E.G.	WR OFF	18/10/43	26	RAAF	CHRISTCHURCH		?
CLEARY	A.E.	SGT	17/08/41		RAF	NOT RECOVERED	221	DID NOT RETURN
COFFEY	J.R.	SGT	28/09/42		RCAF	NOT RECOVERED	7OTU	SEA OFF ST.KILDA
CONNELL	R.D.	OBS U/T	31/10/41	25	RAF(VR)	PRESBYTERIAN CHURCH		OUT OF AN ENGLISH A/F
COOPER	J.D.	SGT	02/01/43	22	RAF?	?	7OTU	LOUGH FOYLE
COOPER	R.G.	SGT	03/04/43	21	RAF?	?	7OTU	OVERSHOT RUNWAY
DEAR		P/O	12/03/41			NOT RECOVERED	502	GALWAY BAY
DESCHAMPS	J.A.	F/SGT WOP/AG	24/10/43	19	RCAF	St.MARY'S	86	LOUGH FOYLE (LIB)
DU PEN		SGT	05/05/43			UK?	7OTU	DRENAGH
EARLE	A.E.	SGT	17/08/41	22	RAF(VR)	NOT RECOVERED	221	DID NOT RETURN
EAVES		SGT	05/05/43			UK?	7OTU	DRENAGH
EDWARDS		P/O	12/03/41			NOT RECOVERED	502	GALWAY BAY
EDWARDS	R.	P/O	11/07/41	32	RAF(VR)	NOT RECOVERED	221	SHOT DOWN
FLETCHER	C.J.	F/SGT	17/08/41	23	RAF(VR)	NOT RECOVERED	221	DID NOT RETURN
FRASER	E.E.	SGT P	12/04/42	29	RAF(VR)	CHRISTCHURCH	1527	CROCKANEEL

Wings Over The Foyle

								44 (FC)
FRY	W.B.	FL SGT	26/09/42	22	RCAF	CHRISTCHURCH FROM ALDER/G	504	(SPITFIRE) DUNGIVEN
FUGILL	D.H.	SGT	17/08/41	25	RAF(VR)	NOT RECOVERED	221	DID NOT RETURN
GARTIER		SGT	28/09/42		RCAF	NOT RECOVERED	7OTU	SEA OFF ST.KILDA
GAULDIN	S.D.	F/O P	05/10/44	30	RAF	CHRISTCHURCH	172	SALTHILL GALWAY
GILLIAN	R.H.	F/SGT	06/03/45	27	RAAF	St.MARY'S		?
GOODLET		SGT	12/03/41			NOT RECOVERED	502	GALWAY BAY
GREENWOOD		SGT	23/01/41			NOT RECOVERED	502	BUNCRANA L/FOYLE
GUTTERRIDGE	R.W.	SGT WOP/AG	28/02/43		RAF(VR)	CHRISTCHURCH	7OTU	GORTAHORK DONEGAL
HAMMOND	A.D.	SGT P	02/01/43	29	RAF?	?	7OTU	LOUGH FOYLE
HARRISON	H.J.B.	SGT WOP/AG	09/10/42	22	RAF(VR)	CHRISTCHURCH	7OTU	LOUGH FOYLE
HIGHFIELD	E.	SGT	31/01/43	23	RAAF	?	7OTU	NIGHT LANDING
HILL		SGT	17/05/43			?	7OTU	LOUGH FOYLE
HINDMARSH	J.	P/O	13/07/43	28	RAF?	?	7OTU	DICKEY GLEN
HOGG		SGT	23/01/41		RAF	NOT RECOVERED	502	BUNCRANA L/FOYLE
HOLDEN		SGT P	05/05/43			UK ?	7OTU	DRENAGH
HOLMES		F/O	23/01/41			?	502	CAMPBELTOWN
HOOK	J.C.	SGT	02/01/43	22	RAF?	?	7OTU	LOUGH FOYLE
HOOKER		SGT	23/01/41			?	502	CAMPBELTOWN
HUCKLESBY	S.	SGT	12/08/42		RAF?	?	7OTU	COAL HILL
HUGES	J.W.	F/SGT	13/07/43	27	RNZAF	St.MARY'S	7OTU	DICKEY GLEN

138

Wings Over The Foyle

		WOP/AG					
HUTTON	E.R.	SGT	28/09/42		RCAF	NOT RECOVERED	7OTU	SEA OFF ST KILDA
JACK	D.H.M.	P/O	11/07/41	24	RAF(VR)	NOT RECOVERED	221	SHOT DOWN
JOHNSON	A.O.	P/O	22/06/41	28	RAF	NOT RECOVERED	221	DID NOT RETURN
JOHNSTON		SGT	23/01/41			?	502	BUNCRANA; L/FOYLE
JONES	D	SGT	23/08/41			?	502	MYROE
LANGHAM	M.R.	F/SGT	12/04/42		RAF?	?	1527	CROCKANEEL 44 (FC)
LOWMAN	D	SGT	02/01/43	21	RAF?	?	7OTU	SISTRAKEEL
MACDOUGALL	J.W.	F/O INSTR MID.	12/04/42	22	RAF(VR)	CHRISTCHURCH	1527	CROCKANEEL 44 (FC)
MacDOWELL	L.P.	SGT(BELFAST)	11/07/41		RAF(VR)	NOT RECOVERED	221	SHOT DOWN
MACINTOSH		SGT	05/05/43			UK ?	7OTU	DRENAGH
MARSHALL	A.S.	SGT	22/06/41	21	RAF(VR)	NOT RECOVERED	221	DID NOT RETURN
MATSON	F.A.	CAPT P	12/04/42	27	RAF(FC)	CHRISTCHURCH	1527	CROCKANEEL 44 (FC)
MATTHEWS		P/O	23/08/41			?	502	MYROE
MATTHEWS	R.H.	P/O(P) R141374	14/02/44	20	RCAF	CHRISTCHURCH	407	STALLED AFTER T/O
McCREADY		SGT	17/05/43			?	7OTU	LOUGH FOYLE
MILLAR	P.T.	SGT	07/12/40			?	502	15 MIN FROM AERODROME
MILSOM	W.W.	P/O P	31/01/43	20	RAF?	?	7OTU	NIGHT LANDING
MONTAGUE	J.L.	P/O	11/04/41		RAF	BEACONSFIELD	221	URRIS HILLS

139

Wings Over The Foyle

MORGAN	K.W.	SGT	22/06/41	21	RAF(VR)	NOT RECOVERED	221	DID NOT RETURN
NAYLOR		SGT	23/08/41			?	502	MYROE
NEILL	F.G.	SGT	11/04/41	22	RAF(VR)	BEDALE	221	URRIS HILLS
NEWEY	N.R.	SGT	12/05/41		RAF(VR)	NOT RECOVERED	221	LOUGH FOYLE
NEWMAN		SGT	05/05/43			UK ?	7OTU	DRENAGH
NEWTON		SGT	17/05/43		RAF?	?	7OTU	LOUGH FOYLE
NO POSITIVE ID			14/02/44		RAF?	?	407	STALLED AFTER TAKE/O
NO POSITIVE ID			14/02/44		RAF?	?	407	STALLED AFTER TAKE/O
NO POSITIVE ID			14/02/44		RAF?	?	407	STALLED AFTER TAKE/O
NORRIS	K.A.	P/O P	17/09/43	23	RCAF	CHRISTCHURCH	7OTU	SCAWL HILL
OATWAY	J.E.	SGT	28/09/42		RCAF	NOT RECOVERED	7OTU	SEA OFF ST.KILDA
ORR		SGT	17/05/43			?	7OTU	LOUGH FOYLE
PAYNE	V.S.	SGT	11/07/41	22	RAF(VR)	NOT RECOVERED	221	SHOT DOWN
PENNINGTON	K.R.	P/O P	02/01/43	26	RAF?	?	7OTU	LOUGH FOYLE
PERKINS	R.G.L.	SGT	11/07/41	24	RAF	NOT RECOVERED	221	SHOT DOWN
PILLING		SGT	23/01/41			?	502	CAMPBELTOWN
PITHER	V.J.	SGT	20/07/42	28	RAAF	CHRISTCHURCH	7OTU	GAINTS CAUSWAY
RAINS	D.	F/SGT	12/08/42	23	RAF?	?	7OTU	COAL HILL
REES	C.W.	F/L	07/12/40			ALDERGROVE	502	15 MIN FROM AERODROME
REES	J.E.	SGT	17/08/41			?	221	DID NOT RETURN

140

Wings Over The Foyle

RICHARDSON	J.G.	CPL	25/05/45	22	RAF	CHRISTCHURCH NORTHAMPTON	281	NO CRASH REC.
ROBERTS-BROWN	R.L.	P/O	12/05/41		RAF(VR)	NORTHAMPTON	221	LOUGH FOYLE
ROBINSON	J.	F/O	12/05/41	23	RAF.AF	NOT RECOVERED	221	LOUGH FOYLE
RUEMPLLER	D.	SGT	02/01/43	21	RAF?	?	7OTU	SISTRAKEEL
SAMUELS	B.	F/SGT	31/01/43	23	RCAF	CARNMONEY JEW CEM	7OTU	NIGHT LANDING
SANDERSON	I.C.M.	F/O	11/07/41	27	RAF(VR)	SCILLY ISLES	221	SHOT DOWN
SMITH	S.A.	FLT/SGT	22/06/41	23	RAF	NOT RECOVERED	221	DID NOT RETURN
SMITH	H.	SGT	02/01/43	21	RAF?	?	7OTU	LOUGH FOYLE
SMITH	E.H.	F/O	03/04/43	23	RAF?	?	7OTU	OVERSHOT RUNWAY
SPROULE		F/O	23/08/41			?	502	MYROE
TAIT	J.	F/O P	13/07/43	23	RAF?	?	7OTU	DICKEY GLEN
TURNBULL	R.A.F.	SGT WOP/AG	02/01/43	22	RAF(VR)	CHRISTCHURCH	7OTU	SISTRAKEEL
TWENTYMAN	W.	P/O P	20/07/42	26	RNZAF	CHRISTCHURCH	7OTU	GAINTS CAUSWAY
TYLER	A.E.	P/O NAV	02/01/43	21	RAF?	?	7OTU	LOUGH FOYLE
WALSH	J.J.	F/SGT	05/11/43	20	RAAF	St.MARY'S	7OTU	EAST OF LIMAVADY
WEEKS	G.V.	P/O	14/11/44	30	RAAF	CHRISTCHURCH		
WHALLEY	F.K.B.	SGT	11/04/41	19	RAF(VR)	LEMMINGTON	221	URRIS HILLS
WHITE	S.G.	SGT	12/05/41	21	RAF(VR)	NOT RECOVERED	221	LOUGH FOYLE
WHITE	T.S.	SGT	28/09/42		RAF	NOT RECOVERED	7OTU	SEA OFF St.KILDA
WIGHMAN	R.P.	SGT WOP/AG	02/01/43	20	RAF(VR)	St.MARY'S	7OTU	SISTRAKEEL

141

Wings Over The Foyle

WILLIS	J.S.	FLT/SGT	22/06/41	25	RAF	NOT RECOVERED	221	DID NOT RETURN
WOODS	L.	F/SGT	28/11/43	29	RAAF	CHRISTCHURCH	7OTU?	PORTBALLINTR AE?
WORTHINGTON	M.I.	P/O	07/12/40			?	502	15 MIN FROM AERODROME
WYNN	C.S.	FLT/SGT	12/05/41	21	RAF	NOT RECOVERED	221	LOUGH FOYLE

Wings Over The Foyle

Top; Limavady Airfield from the air, Lough Foyle in the background.(John Quinn)

Bottom; Limavady's Christchurch and place of honor for those who did not go home.

143

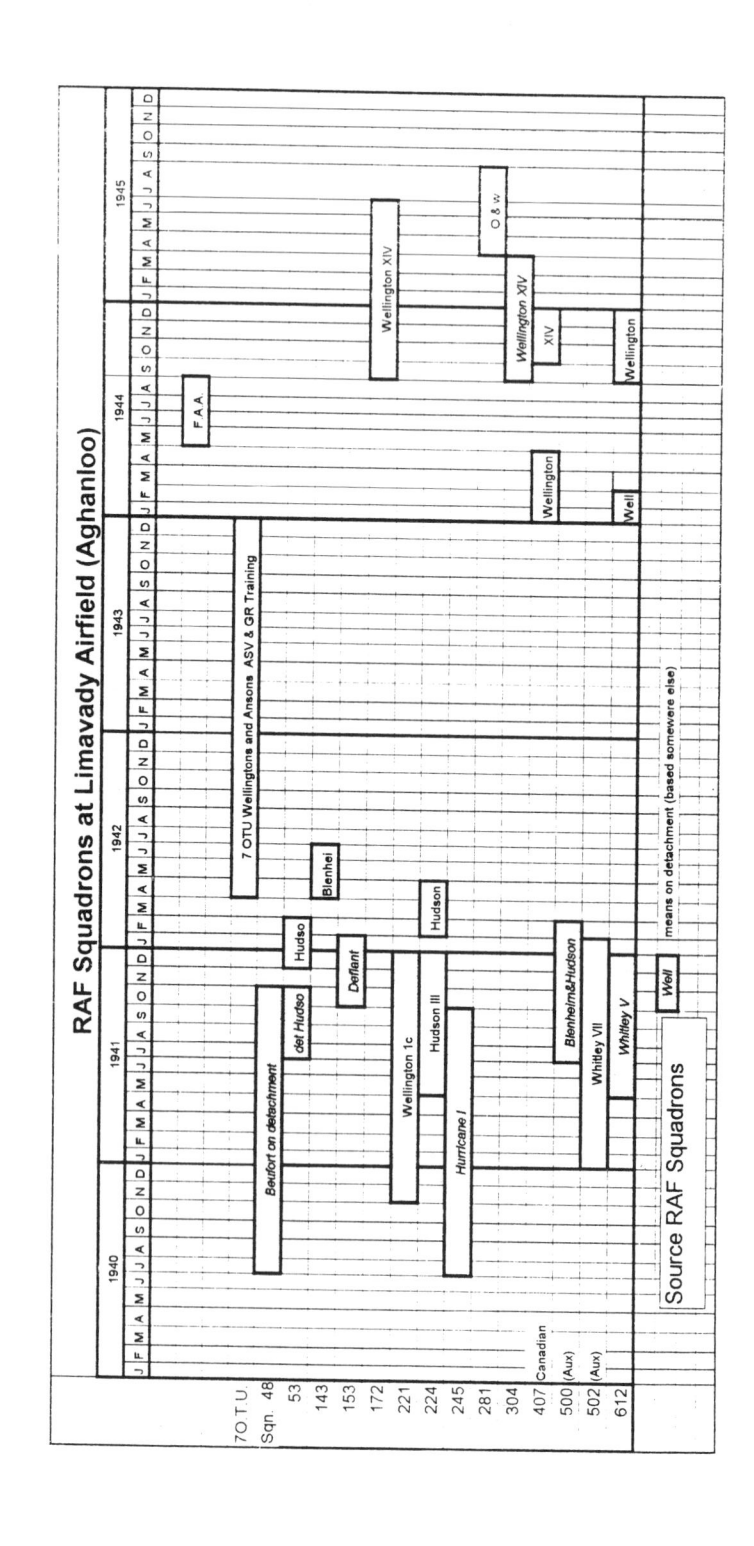

RAF Squadrons at Limavady Airfield (Aghanloo)

Sqn.	1940	1941	1942	1943	1944	1945
7 O T U			7 OTU Wellingtons and Ansons ASV & GR Training			
48	Beaufort on detachment					
53		det Hudso				
143		Hudso				
153		Defiant				
172		Wellington 1c				
221		Hurricane I	Hudson III	Hudson		
224						
245						
281			Blenheim & Hudson		F A A	Wellington XIV	Wellington XIV	O & W
304		Whitley VII				XIV
407 Canadian		Whitley V			Wellington	Wellington
500 (Aux)		Well			Well	
502 (Aux)						
612						

Source RAF Squadrons

means on detachment (based somewhere else)

BOMB STORES
18
13
09
27
31
36
A.M. BOUNDARY SHEWN THUS
SCALE OF FEET

References

221 Squadron Old Comrades Magazine	Various	221 Squadron Association
221 Squadron Operation Records		Public Records London.
245 Squadron Operation Records		Public Records London.
502 Squadron Operation Records		Public Records London.
Action Stations. Vol 7	D. J. Smith.	Patrick Stephens Limited 1989.
Archives Dept		RAF Museum Hendon.
Britians Sea War.	J. M. Young.	Patrick Stephens Limited 1989.
Guinness Book Of Aircraft.	Mondey & Taylor	Guinness Publishing Ltd 1988.
RAF Squadron	Wing Commander C.G..Jefford	Airlife England
Scourge Of The Atlantic:	Kenneth Poolman:	Book Clubs Associates London 1979
Twenty-One Squadrons	Leslie Hunt	Garnstone Press
Ulster Airmail	Various	Ulster Aviation Society.
Wartime Air Crashes And Forced Landings In County Donegal	John Quinn	Irish Wreckology Group Publication 1993

Index.

2
272 Squadron • 21, 27, 28

4
407 Squadron • 20, 23

5
59 Squadron • 17, 83, 88

6
612 Squadron • 22, 107

A
Aldergrove • 9, 14, 16, 21, 25, 27, 28, 29, 99, 101, 103, 106, 108, 117, 123
Alexander Arms • 17, 79
ASV • 15, 16, 21, 22, 27, 30, 35, 38, 41, 48, 55, 56, 57, 60, 61, 62, 63, 72, 73, 84, 86, 97, 102, 103, 109, 113, 116, 122

B
Bancroft • 87
Barber • 3, 97
Bateman • 50, 51
Berehaven • 14
Bevan • 29, 117, 118
Billings • 28
Bismarck • 25, 40
Bliss • 38, 96
Brock • 106, 107, 117
Bulloch • 39

C
Cakebread • 22, 39
Carmichael • 100, 101, 116
Cattley • 1, 9, 38, 47, 49, 50, 63, 67, 71, 72, 73, 74
Cave • 31, 88
Churchill • 6, 13
Cobh • 14
Collie • 99, 118, 119
Corry • 32, 108, 109, 116, 117

D
Dear • 29, 115, 116
Derby House • 14, 35
Dickson • 3, 33, 76, 99, 100, 101, 102, 115, 116
Douglas • 3, 89, 91, 97, 115
Drenagh • 15, 79, 81, 85, 87, 104
Dunree • 3, 45, 46, 64, 67, 74

147

E
Everett • 107

G
Gorteen • 85, 87
Grant • 3, 79, 88, 93, 97, 124

H
H.M.S. Maplin • 107
H.M.S. Wescott • 107
Hill • 25, 122
Hinkley • 27
Holdsworth • 21, 30, 31
Hoskins • 40
Huston • 3, 86

I
Inishtrahul • 56
Irvine • 80

J
Jefferson • 114, 121, 122
Johnson P/O • 22, 39
Johnston • 30, 114, 121, 122

K
Kretschmer • 35

L
Leigh • 15, 38, 39, 40
Lindsay • 108, 117

M
Malin Head • 45, 56
McBratney • 15, 39
McGiffin • 3, 27, 32, 33, 39, 102, 103, 113
McLeod • 107, 117
Millar • 3, 89, 114
Montague • 38, 51
Murdock • 40

N
Neill • 52, 53, 54
No.143 Squadron • 16

O
Opitz • 30

P
P3428 • 25
Parr • 34
Paytner • 23
Pearce • 36, 101, 116
Pike • 3, 17, 83
Pilar de Larrinaga • 107
Pither • 105, 110
Preston • 29, 115
Prien • 35
Procter • 15, 39

R
Ray • 15, 39
Ricketts • 28, 69
Robinson • 38, 79

S

S.S.Chinese Prince • 83
Sanderson • 22, 39, 74
Scrom • 25
Shore • 107, 117
Southan • 30
Spooner • 1, 3, 6, 15, 16,
 40, 41, 55, 56, 63,
 65, 72, 76, 78, 79,
 80, 82, 83, 84, 88,
 93, 95, 101
Sproule • 29, 117
St. Kilda • 58
Starling E • 3, 15, 37, 42,
 55, 58, 65, 76, 77,
 96
Stewart and Partner • 86
Swilly • 14, 28, 45, 56

T

Tizard • 15
Tory Island • 56
Turner • 87, 91
Twentyman • 105, 110

U

U206 • 30, 120
U545 • 23
U772 • 23
U844 • 17
U93 • 21, 28, 120
Urris • 22, 38, 45, 60, 65,
 67, 74, 75

V

Vickers • 34, 40, 72

W

W5653 • 2, 3, 22, 34, 38,
 44, 45, 48, 55, 56,
 60, 64, 65, 66, 67,
 68, 69, 74, 75, 130
Walker • 21, 28, 35, 120
Ward • 114, 121, 122
Whalley • 51, 67
Wilkinson • 29, 30, 115
Wilson • 3, 89, 90, 104, 110,
 116
Woods • 76, 105, 111, 120

Z

Zigmond • 17, 43